THE EXCAVATION OF A MEDIEVAL RURAL SETTLEMENT AT THE PEPPER HILL LANE ELECTRICITY SUBSTATION, NORTHFLEET, KENT

By Alan Hardy and Chris Bell

With contributions by

Leigh Allen, Kate Atherton, Paul Blinkhorn, Paul Booth, Philippa Bradley, Greg Campbell, Jon Chandler, Bethan Charles, Claire Ingrem and Ruth Pelling

Illustrations by Peter Lorimer

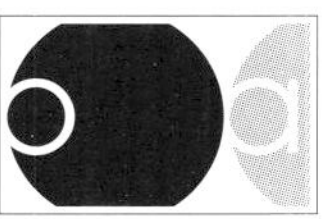

Oxford Archaeology
Occasional Paper Number 10
December 2001

Front cover:
The site during the topsoil stripping, looking west

Back cover:
The medieval phases and the pylon base

ISBN 0-904220-28-1

Typeset by Mathematical Composition Setters Ltd, Salisbury, Wiltshire
Printed by Henry Ling Ltd, Dorchester

Contents

THE EXCAVATION OF A MEDIEVAL RURAL SETTLEMENT AT THE PEPPER HILL LANE ELECTRICITY SUBSTATION, NORTHFLEET, KENT

By Alan Hardy and Chris Bell

With contributions by

Leigh Allen, Kate Atherton, Paul Blinkhorn, Paul Booth, Philippa Bradley, Greg Campbell, Jon Chandler, Bethan Charles, Claire Ingrem and Ruth Pelling

Illustrations by Peter Lorimer

Acknowledgements

The authors would like to thank the National Grid Company, who funded the excavation and publication. Thanks are also due to Ray Russell and Mike Reave of NGC, and the staff of M Daly Plant Hire Ltd, for their assistance and co-operation during the fieldwork. The advice and comments of Wendy Rogers, Archaeological Officer with Kent County Council are gratefully acknowledged. The fieldwork project was managed by Paul Booth and directed on site by Chris Bell. The post-excavation project was managed by Alan Hardy, and the report was edited by Anne Dodd. We are grateful to the following for kindly providing information about comparable sites in Kent in advance of publication: Union Railways (North) Ltd and Wessex Archaeology for the current CTRL excavations at Springhead; Union Railways (South) Ltd and the Canterbury Archaeological Trust for Westenhanger; Union Railways (South) Ltd and the Museum of London Archaeology Service for Northumberland Bottom; Ian Riddler and the Canterbury Archaeological Trust for Monkton. Anne Dodd would like to thank Helen Glass (Rail Link Engineering), Ian Riddler (Canterbury Archaeological Trust), Phil Andrews (Wessex Archaeology), Niall Roycroft (Museum of London Archaeology Service), Stuart Foreman (OAU) and Julian Munby (OAU), who have answered questions and provided most helpful information and ideas during the process of compilation of this report.

Summary

An excavation in 1999 by the Oxford Archaeological Unit on land just north of the line of Watling Street, at the southern edge of the parish of Northfleet, found evidence of medieval occupation and settlement. This took the form of field boundaries, paddocks and vestigial structural remains, dating to the 11th and 12th centuries. It is suggested that this was part of the settlement known as Wenifalle in the late 12th century, which survived as a nearby farm – Wingfield Bank – until the 20th century.

Project background

In 1999, Oxford Archaeological Unit (OAU) carried out a series of archaeological works on land at the Northfleet East Substation, Pepper Hill Lane, Northfleet, Kent (NGR TQ 6230 7245) on behalf of the National Grid Company. The works were required to mitigate the effects of the building of a new electricity substation. OAU carried out an archaeological evaluation of the site in January 1999. This comprised three trenches, machine-excavated in an area of rough pasture immediately to the north of the existing works compound. Of these, the two trenches situated in the central and eastern parts of the area revealed archaeological features and deposits dated by pottery to the 11th and 12th centuries. These medieval features were considered to merit further examination, and a programme of excavation was agreed with Kent County Council. The excavation was carried out in August 1999.

Site Location and Topography

The site lies approximately 2 km south of the core of Northfleet and 100 m north of the present line of the A2, and is bounded by a disused railway to the west and the Southfleet to Northfleet road to the east. Topographically the site is situated on the southwestern edge of a headland overlooking the Ebbsfleet Valley to the west, and the site of the Roman town of Springhead to the southwest.

Geology

The solid geology consists of Cretaceous Upper Chalk, with overlying caps of Palœocene Thanet Beds forming the higher ground. The drift geology for the area is recorded as Pleistocene Head Deposits, principally manifested on the site as pale yellow sand with chalky clay, and coarse flinty gravel which was predominant in the eastern part of the site.

Archaeological Background

The Springhead area has been of interest to antiquarians and archaeologists for at least two hundred years, but that interest has been almost exclusively focused on its prehistoric and Romano-British archaeology. The area contains a number of prehistoric sites, but the vast majority of the finds in the area have been Roman, and substantial work has been carried out in the area of the Roman 'small town' of Vagniacis (Fig. 1). Excavations up to the early 1980s have been summarised by Detsicas (1983, 60–76) and by Burnham and Wacher (1990, 192–198).

As a Roman 'small town', Springhead is best known for its important temple complex, which was situated beside Watling Street. The line of Watling Street follows a marked dogleg through the settlement and its route immediately west of Springhead is unclear (Smith 1997). The settlement appears to have been fairly small, though recent work has indicated that occupation extended south of the nucleus alongside a minor road (Boyle Early 1998; Philp Chenery 1997) and that a major cemetery of some 561 cremations and inhumations lay beside this road to the south of the settlement (Glass 1999, 205–208). At the time of preparation of this report in the winter of 2000–2001, further excavations were underway some 300 m west of the present site, on the far side of the disused railway line, in advance of the Channel Tunnel Rail Link. Preliminary results from this work, carried out by Wessex Archaeology on behalf of Union Railways (North) Ltd, indicate further substantial evidence for Iron Age and Roman activity (P Andrews, pers. comm.).

The archaeological evidence for early medieval occupation in the area is meagre. In 1847 the remains of an Anglo-Saxon cemetery were uncovered on 'the elevated ground at Northfleet' (Smith 1848, 235) during construction of the railway that passes approximately 1 km north of the site. The discoveries included several urns (at least one filled with burnt human bone), iron shield bosses, early forms of saucer brooches and a variety of iron spearheads (Smith 1848, 235–237; Leeds 1913, 115). A number of inhumation burials were also uncovered (Tester 1969, 149). The cemetery is one of a small number of Kentish 'mixed' inhumation/cremation Anglo-Saxon burial grounds situated on the south side of the Thames.

The current work 300 m west of the site (see above) has found a small group of Anglo-Saxon burials, provisionally thought to be of early Saxon date, and two probable grain-drying features, one of which was associated with a coin of the mid 9th century. No features of post-Conquest date had been identified at the time of writing; three coins and a pilgrim's ampulla, all of 13th- to 14th-century date, had been retrieved but appeared to be chance losses perhaps related to activity along Pilgrims' Way.

Figure 1: Site location

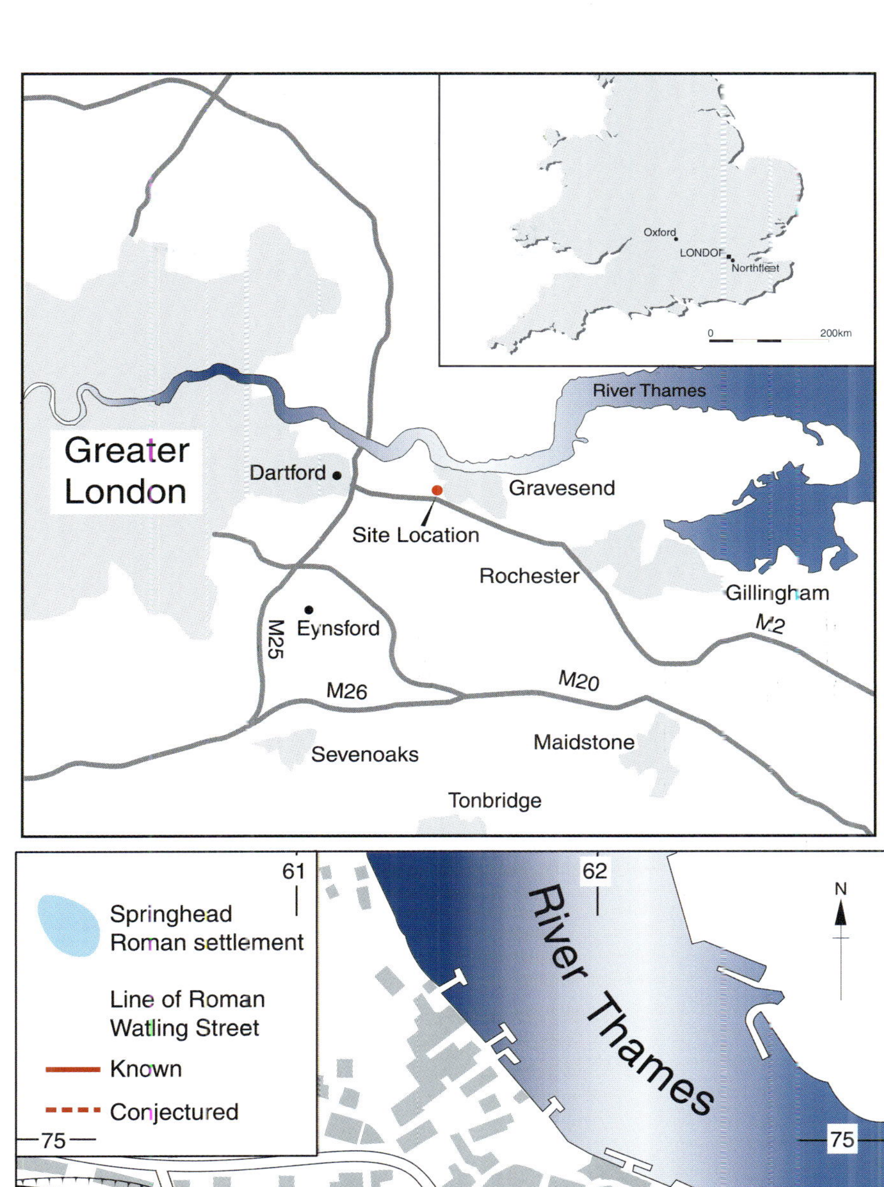

Oxford
LONDON
Northfleet
0 200km
River Thames
Greater London
Dartford
Gravesend
Site Location
Rochester
Gillingham
Eynsford
M2
M25
M26
M20
Sevenoaks
Maidstone
Tonbridge

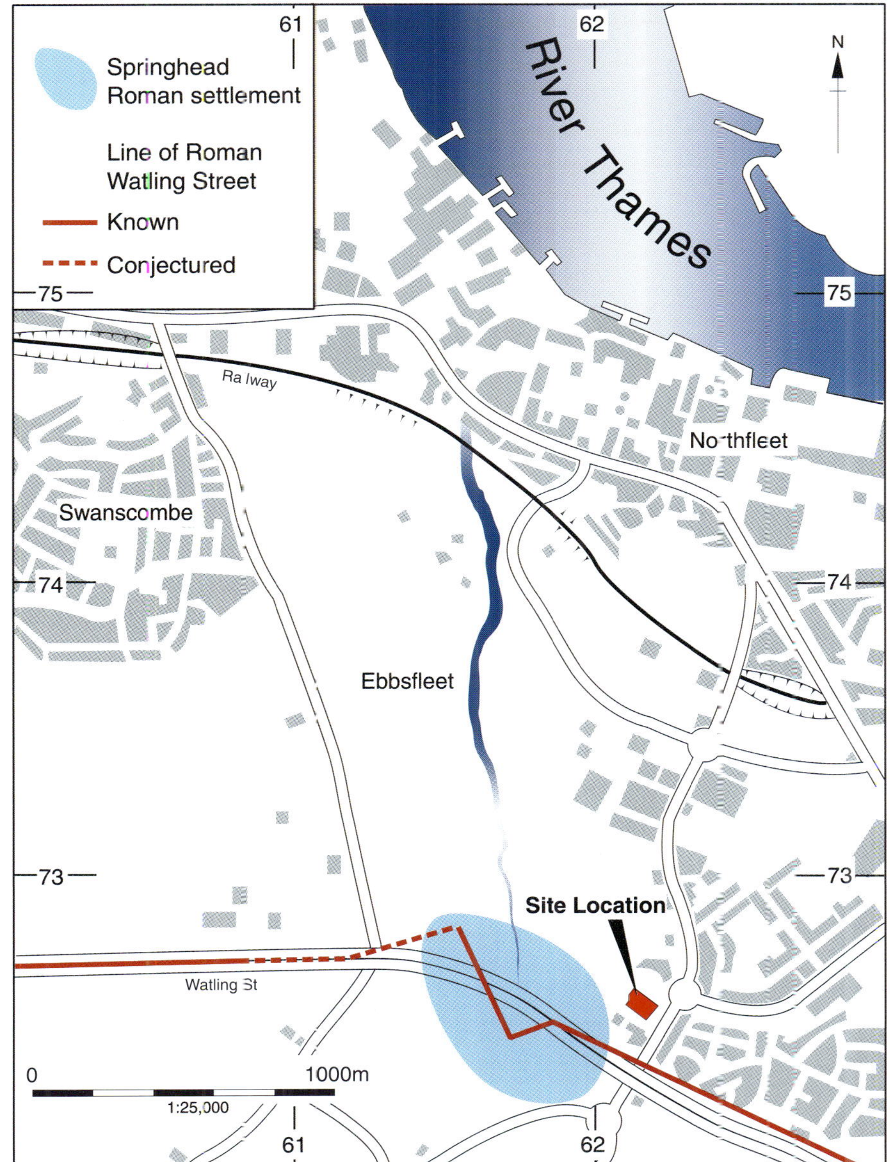

Springhead Roman settlement
Line of Roman Watling Street
Known
Conjectured
River Thames
N
61
62
75
75
Railway
Northfleet
Swanscombe
74
74
Ebbsfleet
73
73
Site Location
Watling St
0 1000m
1:25,000
61
62

Historical Background (Figure 2)
by Jon Chandler

The site lies on the western edge of the ancient parish of Northfleet, which is Old English for '*north river*' (Edwards 1974, 83). The manor, first mentioned in Domesday, was owned by the Archbishop of Canterbury and formed part of the Toltingtrough Hundred. The manor was held from the Archbishop by Richard de Tonbridge 'in his Lowy'. The Lowy was a large discontinuous area of land, the primary purpose of which was to provide resources for the maintenance and defence of Tonbridge Castle 25 km to the south (Dumbreck 1959, 147).

The exact location of settlement, or the manor house (if any) within the manor at the time of Domesday is uncertain. It is likely that the primary focus of settlement was at Northfleet, the historic centre of which is situated approximately 1.75 km to the north of the GIS Substation Site. In the centre of the settlement lies the parish church of St Botolph, almost certainly the church mentioned in Domesday. The building mainly dates to the late 13th-14th century, although it has been suggested that remains in the south-west corner could be from an aisle-less Saxon church (Newman 1969, 419).

Northfleet was one of a number of settlements located in the foothills of the North Downs beside the Thames. The Thames and its tributary the Ebbsfleet would have been primary factors in the choice of the location for the settlement and probably explain why the focus of population is located so far north within the parish, rather than at its centre. Land to the south of the primary settlement would probably have been outlying pasture or woodland extending to the Kentish Downlands to the south (Everitt 1986, 87).

The medieval period (c12th – 16th century)

The Tithe Map of Northfleet dated 1838 is the earliest detailed map of the study area (see Fig. 2). No buildings are shown on the site, which is located in field no. 412, at the north-east corner of which is 'Wingfield Bank', a large farm comprising at least four buildings at the side of the road leading from Watling Street northwards towards Northfleet. The place-name is derived from *Wenifalle* meaning 'a leap or tract of fallen trees blown by wind' or simply 'windy field' (Wallenberg 1934, 107).

Wingfield Bank (or *Wenifalle*) is first mentioned in documentary sources dating to the first year of the reign of King John (1199) when the Archbishop of Canterbury and his clerk 'freely and without any dispute gave up to the use of the monks [of Rochester Priory] the tithes [amongst other landholdings in Northfleet] of Wenifalle' (Hasted 1797, 316). The reference suggests that at this time there was a distinct landholding at Wingfield Bank, and implies that there was settlement there. The settlement continued in existence throughout the medieval period as the place-name Winefeld/Wyndfeld (there are numerous minor variations in spelling) and is mentioned in documentary sources throughout the 13th and 14th centuries (Wallenberg 1934, 107).

The settlement at Wingfield Bank would have been an early form of secondary settlement located some distance from the primary settlement around the green at Northfleet. Why a settlement was established here is not clear but it is possibly associated with the continued use of Watling Street, which served as the primary road from London to Dover via Canterbury during the Roman period. The road probably continued as an important line of communication for some time after the Roman period although it eventually declined in significance (see below).

An indication of the general settlement pattern in the area in the later medieval period is provided by early maps of the area. The earliest of these are a map of Northfleet produced in Hasted's history of Kent published in 1799, and the Ordnance Survey field drawings that same year. Aside from Northfleet itself the

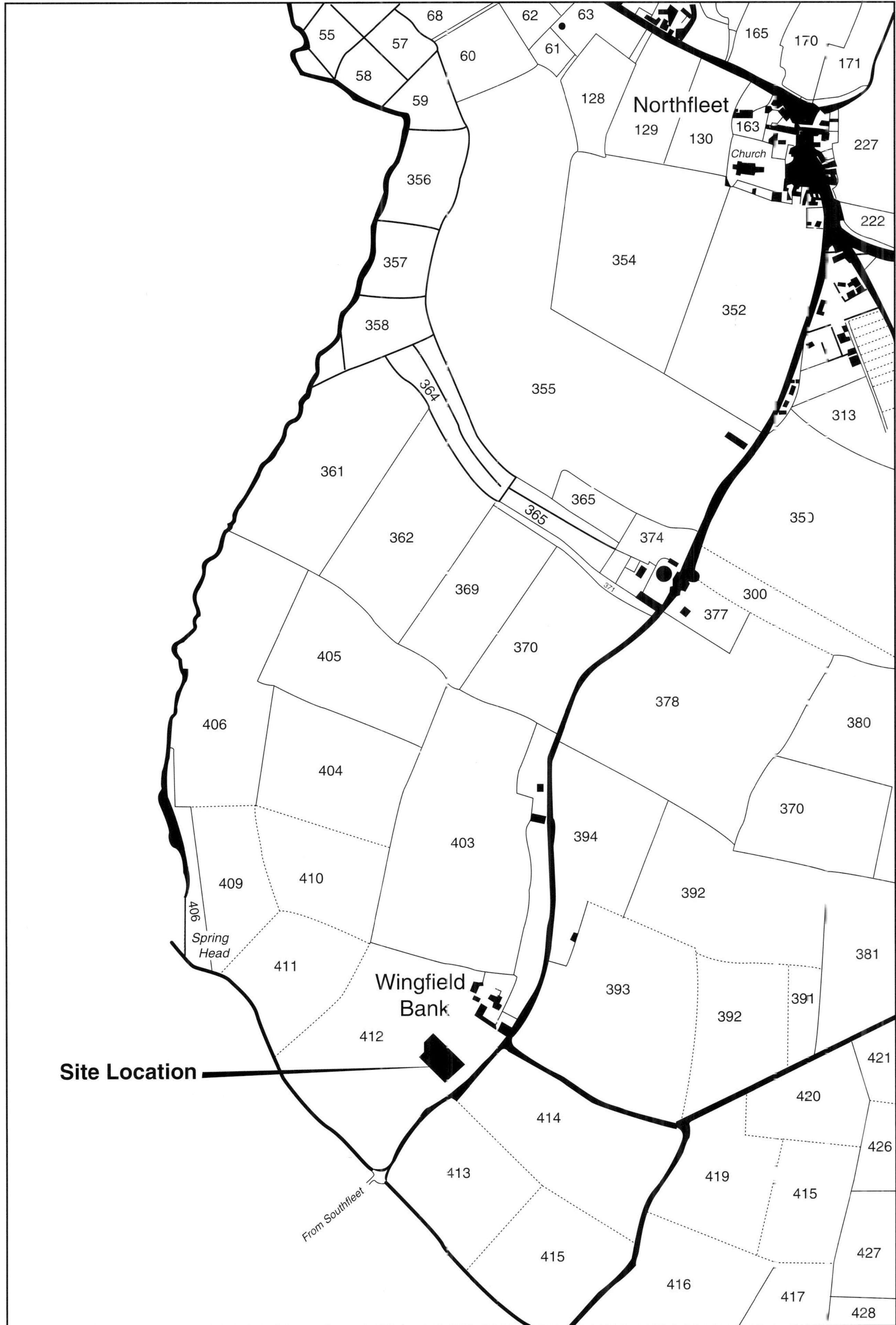

Scale 1:10,560 - 6" 1mile

Figure 2: Detail from 1838 Tithe Map of Northfleet

remainder of the parish is thinly populated, with a few secondary settlements, Perry Street and Parsonage to the south and south-east. Both maps show the site of Wingfield Bank farmstead in its modern position (prior to modern redevelopment – see below), c 100 m to the north-east of the GIS Substation Site.

In the later medieval period the importance of Watling Street as the main route from London to Canterbury, Dover and the continent declined considerably, probably due to the growth in importance of Gravesend from the mid 13th century onward. From at least 1293 Gravesend served as a port or 'Long Ferry' from London to the continent (Hiscock 1969, 229). The principal road now deviated from Watling Street at a point east of Dartford, c 7 km west of the site, and headed eastwards towards Gravesend, via Northfleet, rather than continuing on a south-east alignment. Beyond Gravesend the road ran to the south-east and rejoined Watling Street at Strood, beside the crossing of the Medway, c 10 km to the south-east of the site. Such a development might explain the relative lack of historic settlement along the 'redundant' section of Watling Street as indicated by early OS maps.

Post-medieval and modern development (c 16th–20th century)

Little changed in the general distribution and occupation centres of the parish of Northfleet until the second half of the 18th century. The 1838 Tithe Map for Northfleet (Fig. 2) and the OS 1st edition 6″ map (1869–73) show the farmstead of Wingfield (Winfield) Bank remaining fairly isolated and there are no other settlements close by.

In the 1920s the new A2 re-established the line of Watling Street, a feature which has consequently come to dominate the local landscape for a second time. Modern OS maps show sprawling development in the northern and central parts of Northfleet parish, primarily associated with the expansion southwards of Gravesend. This development has absorbed the smaller settlements, such as Perry Street, but as yet the area of the site between the Ebbsfleet and the B2175 (connecting the A2 to Northfleet) has remained relatively free of modern development. In more recent times the site of Wingfield Bank was redeveloped as a supermarket.

The excavation

Methodology (Figure 3)

The area designated for excavation, determined on the basis of the evaluation results, encompassed approximately 3,600 sq m of the eastern half of the development area. As this area included the base of a standing electricity pylon, an area of approximately 450 sq m was rendered inaccessible to excavation for reasons of Health and Safety.

An average depth of 0.40 m of topsoil and post-medieval/modern ploughsoil was stripped using a mechanical excavator equipped with a toothless ditching bucket.

Removal of the topsoil and plough soil revealed the soil marks of negative features in the sand and gravel of the subsoil. Excavation was selective; intersections of linear features were excavated, as were terminals and comparative sections along their lengths. Three large pit features were excavated by quadrant and/or section and ultimately fully excavated. Discrete postholes and pits were at least half-sectioned. Some very shallow and indistinct features near the eastern edge of the site were recorded on plan but not excavated. All archaeological recording followed standard OAU practice (Wilkinson 1992).

A strategy of selective bulk sampling for environmental remains was pursued, with samples taken from deposits within the large sunken features and other features containing concentrations of occupation debris.

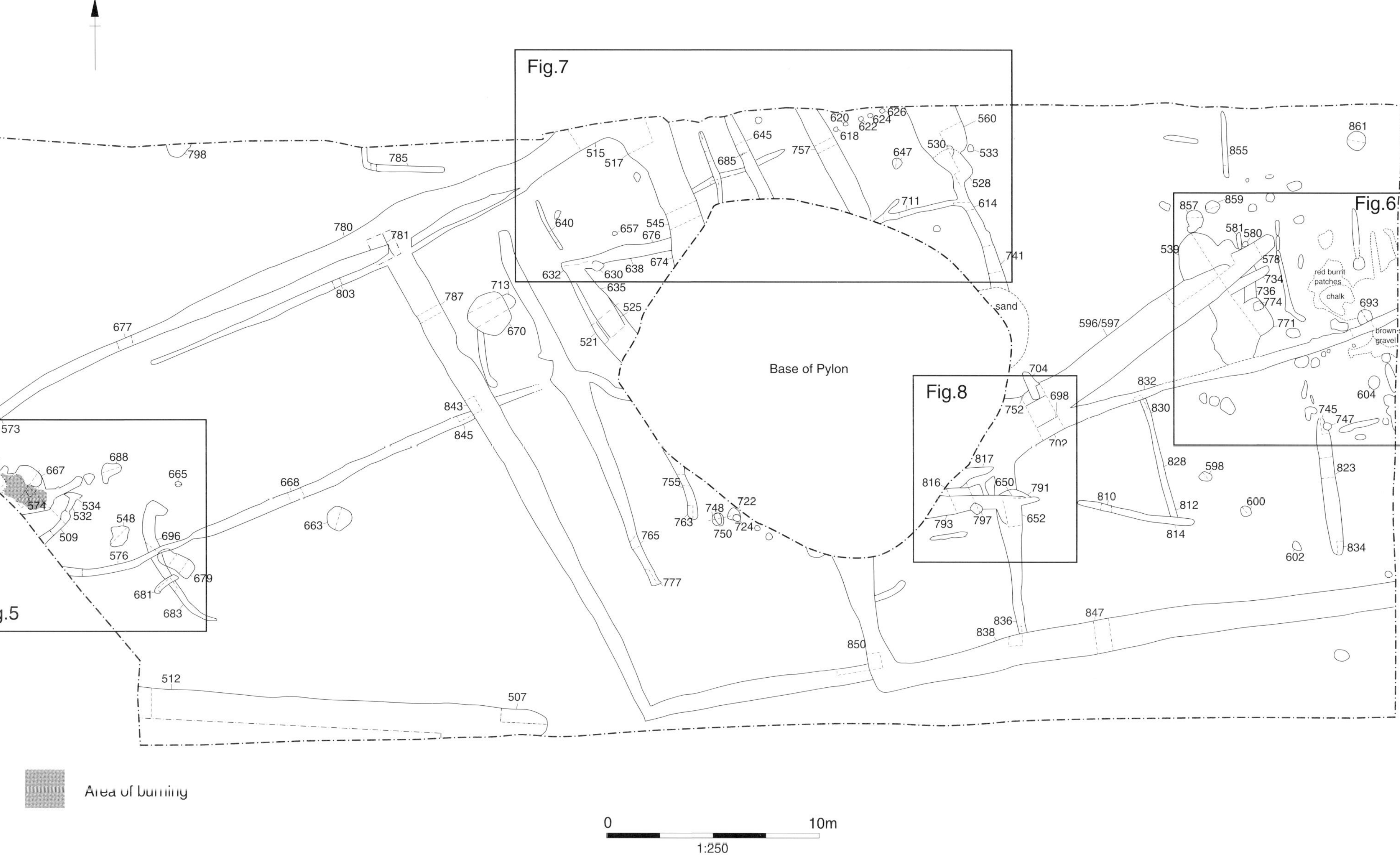

Figure 3: Overall site plan showing excavated areas and location of detail figures

RESULTS   **General**

The clarity of observed stratigraphic relationships was variable; proximity to foci of occupation tended to result in darker feature fills and more distinct interfaces, both between features and between features and the natural subsoil. Where features were situated further from such foci, the interface with the natural subsoil in plan and section was sometimes difficult to establish.

A second factor affecting the interpretation of the archaeological sequence was the degree of post-occupational truncation by ploughing, which varied across the site, partly due to the gradient of the slope and partly to the character of the underlying subsoil. The coarse gravelly subsoil of the eastern part of the site appeared to have been more seriously scoured resulting in severe damage to already insubstantial features in this area.

The phasing (Figure 4)

The chronological phasing is based primarily on the stratigraphic relationships determined on site, and apparent spatial relationships between physically unrelated features or groups of features. Features that were artefactually undated and/or lacked stratigraphic relationships were phased according to plausible spatial relationships, or, in the case of ditches, by similarities of feature size, shape and fill. The pottery was too closely tied to a short chronological period to be of use in refining the chronology. It should be noted, therefore, that there is still a degree of uncertainty about the precise phasing of some features; the authors suggest the phasing scheme below as the likeliest interpretation.

Phasing Summary

Phase 1 Late 11th to early 12th century
Phase 2 Early to mid 12th century
Phase 3 Mid to late 12th century

Archaeological Description (Figures 3–9)

Phase 1

The earliest identified activity on the site was represented by three concentrations of features, comprising pits, postholes, ditches and gullies. The first group was concentrated against the western edge of the site, but extended to the north-east and may have linked with the second group, situated against the northern edge of excavation. The third group was situated against the eastern side of the site.

The western group (Figures 3 and 5)
The focus of activity in the western group was a shallow flat-bottomed feature (554), defining an approximate semicircle against the western edge of the site. It was filled by a burnt surface made up of compacted chalk, clay and soil (531), possibly representing a hearth or even the truncated base of an oven or kiln. An irregular feature (573) extended to the south east, covering an area of approximately 5 sq m. A sample section revealed a shallow ditch-like profile with a north-south orientation, containing an accumulation of lenses of burnt clay, charcoal and sand, but no artefactual evidence (see Fig. 9, Section 69). A posthole (667), apparently contemporary with 573, was also identified.

Immediately south of 573 was a shallow beam slot (509) extending in a slight curve from the western baulk. The slot measured 0.40 m wide × 0.13 m deep, and at least one posthole was seen to be associated with the slot (Fig. 9, Section 53) – although it was not recorded separately. The fill of the beamslot produced a number of fragments of fired clay, some with wattle marks which suggest that the structure originally consisted of wattle-and-daub infilling within a wooden frame.

Figure 4: Interpretative Phase plan

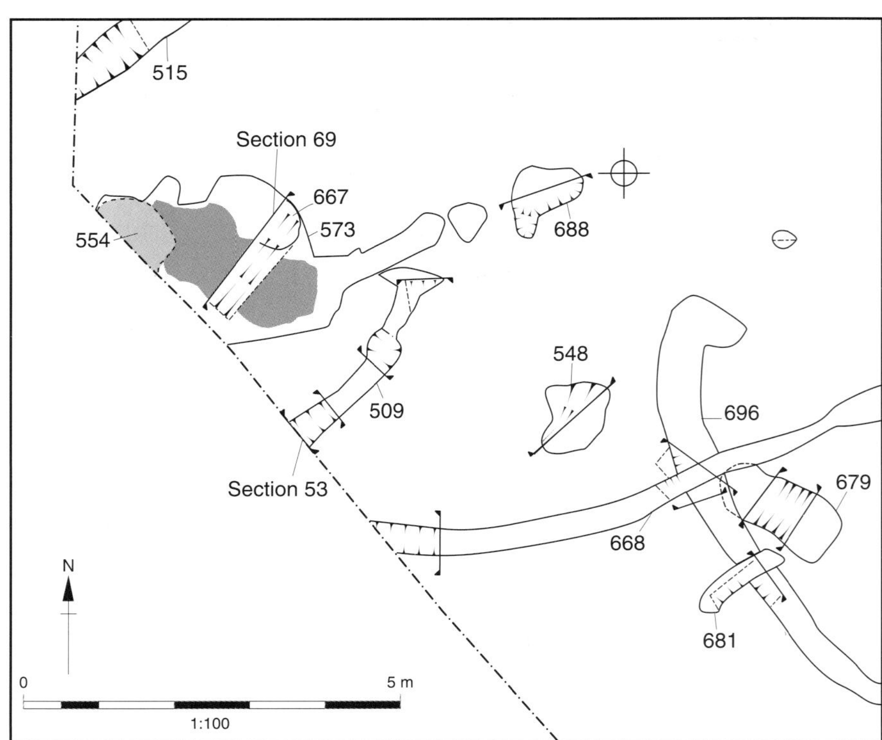

Figure 5: Detail plan of western area

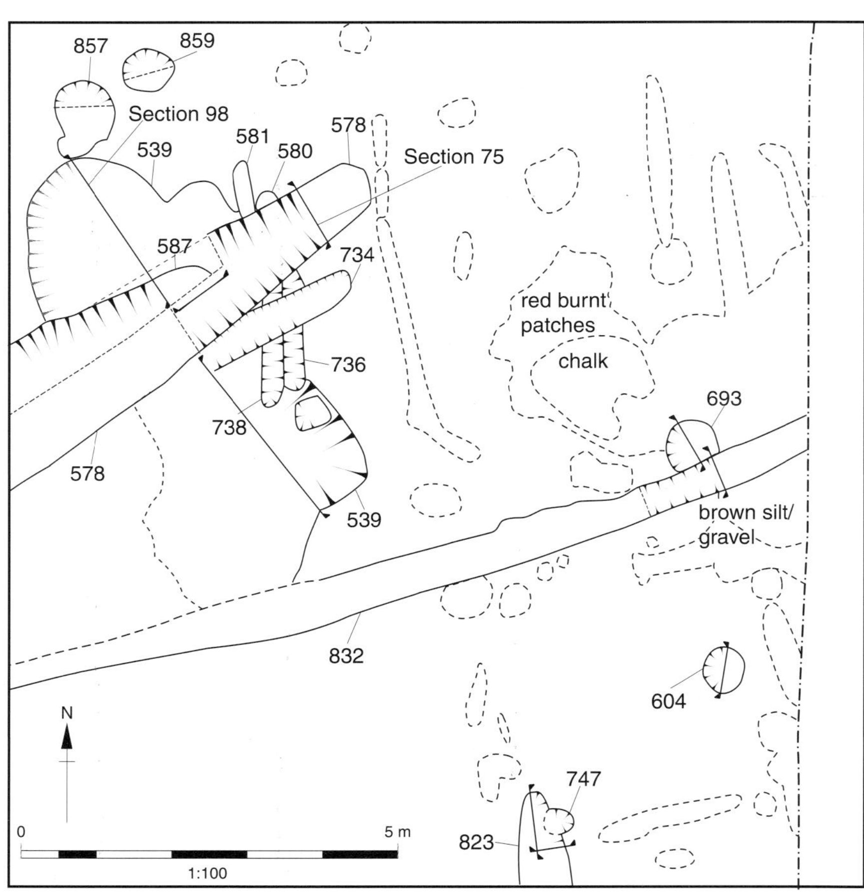

Figure 6: Detail plan of eastern area

A number of other features were identified to the south and east of the beamslot, including three shallow pits (688, 548, and 663 – not illustrated) and a curving linear feature (696). Although their function is unclear, their association with the possible oven activity to the north is indicated by the relatively high percentage of charcoal and burnt clay observed within their fills.

The curving gully 696 was cut by a NE-SW gully (668) that extended from the west baulk for a distance of approximately 34 m, before petering out. It averaged 0.75 m wide × 0.15 m deep with a shallow bowl-shaped profile. A parallel gully of similar proportions (803) was identified 11 m to the north of 668, extending approximately 28 m to a point where it was truncated by later activity (see Fig. 4). A small quantity of pottery was recovered from the fill (577) of the western end of gully 563.

While this part of the site was clearly the focus of much activity, it did not seem to involve the use or disposal of pottery or animal bone, judging by the meagre assemblage recovered.

The eastern group (Figures 3 and 6)
This group comprised a spread of features on the eastern side of the site, the largest of which was a sub-rectangular shallow hollow (539) measuring approximately 8.3 m long by 4.0 m wide and averaging 0.3 m deep. The definition of the south-western quarter of the feature was noticeably indistinct in plan. The central part of 539 was heavily truncated by the ditch termini of phase 2 (see Fig. 9 Section 98), but, where not disturbed, the fills of 539 were generally silty sand/gravel (540), overlain by grey sandy silt (541), neither fill producing any finds. The eastern side of 539 was cut by two north-south gullies (581/738 and 734) each approximately 5 m long. A similarly oriented small gully (855), possibly representing a beamslot, was located 3.5 m to the north (see Fig. 3).

A spread of very indistinct and shallow features on a similar alignment, and at right-angles to it, were identified in plan at intervals to the east, close to the eastern baulk (these are shown as dotted lines on Figs. 3 and 6). The form and layout of these features strongly suggests the vestigial remains of a building, measuring 10 × 4 m internally, orientated NNW/SSE. The beamslots survived as shallow linear features, and the postholes as shallow circular depressions. Two postholes halfway along the west side of the building, set 1 m apart, suggest an entrance, and immediately to the south in the interior of the building are soil marks that suggest there may have been a partition here, dividing the structure into two distinct rooms. Patches of chalk and small areas of burning in the northern half of the building suggest the presence of a hearth. The function of the southern half of the building is not apparent from the surviving remains, although posthole 604 could have supported a loft over half the room, increasing its capacity for storage. Two sherds of pottery (see Medieval Pottery, below) were recovered from the fill (605) of this posthole; the sherds were in Early Medieval Sand and Shell Ware (Museum of London code EMSS), equivalent to the 'Sandy-shelly' fabric from Dartford. This pottery is considered by Blinkhorn (below) to be consistent with a late 11th – to mid 12th-century date.

A north-south gully (823, see Figs. 3 and 6) ran southwards from this group, on the same alignment. It was 9.2 m long × 1.0 m wide × 0.45 m deep. A posthole (747) was located at its northern end, but is probably to be associated with the building. A short length of gully (828, see Fig. 3) on a similar alignment was situated approximately 7 m to the west of 823. Both termini of the gully were truncated by later activity. A line of three postholes or small pits (598, 600, 602, see Fig. 3) lay between the two gullies. Each was no more than 0.12 m deep and none produced any finds from their sandy silt fills.

A further scatter of features was identified to the north of this area, including three pits (857, 859 and 861 – Fig. 3) each approximately 1.0 m in diameter and between 0.15 m and 0.25 m deep. The pit fills were a similar grey brown sandy silt, and produced a small quantity of pottery. The pits and a scatter of possible postholes (recorded in plan but not excavated) appeared to be on the same alignment as the recut ditch (578) of phase 2.

The northern group (Figures 3 and 7)
The group consisted of a concentration of features to the north of the pylon base.

The earliest feature (560) was a shallow subrectangular hollow, partially revealed against the north baulk and measuring approximately 4.0 m × 3.0 m in plan, with an average depth of 0.32 m. A shallow bowl-shaped feature (530) was identified in the base of 560, and another shallow depression (533) was recorded immediately to the east of the hollow. The south end of feature 560 was truncated by a pit (528), measuring 2.2 m west-east × 3.0 m north-south, with a maximum depth of 0.80 m.

The lower fills of these features were fairly consistent, being grey brown sandy silts with flecks of charcoal. A total of 17 sherds of pottery were recovered from the fills of the north-west quadrant of the hollow 560, far more than were recovered from the other three quadrants, which may suggest that a focus for activity lay to the north-west of the feature.

A single posthole or small pit (647) was located 2.0 m west of hollow 560, measuring 0.59 m in diameter × 0.21 m deep. The single fill (648) was a silty sand and gravel and was devoid of finds.

A series of features extended westwards from hollow 560 on a consistent WSW-ENE alignment. Five postholes (618, 620, 622, 624 and 626) aligned NE-SW ran for a length of 2.5 m from the west side of the hollow. They were of similar dimensions, approximately 0.22 m-0.26 m in diameter and between 0.10 m and 0.15 m deep, and had similar fills of sandy silt, with inclusions of small limestone pieces that might represent the remains of post-packing. No finds were recovered from any of the postholes. Unfortunately the relationship between the posthole line and the hollow can only be inferred as any intersection and evidence of stratigraphic relationship would have occurred beyond the edge of the trench.

A shallow gully (710), surviving to a length of 6.90 m and 0.34 m wide × 0.10 m deep, was located to the south-west of the posthole line, and on the same alignment. The western terminus of the gully was truncated by a large later ditch (545, see phase 3 below). Gully 710 was bisected at right-angles by two other linear features. Gully 708, of similar dimensions to 710, extended for a length of approximately 5.1 m from a terminus close to the northern baulk to the edge of the pylon base. The other linear feature (645) was clearly of later date and is described below (phase 2).

Two postholes (657 and 660) both measuring approximately 0.30 m in diameter × 0.30 m deep, were identified further to the west, on the same alignment. A short length of gully (640) extended from just beyond the western posthole (660) to a point close to the terminus of gully 803 (phase 1 western group; this relationship is shown most clearly on Fig. 4).

Phase 2

The principal activity of phase 2 comprised a sub-rectangular enclosure, apparently centred on the site of the pylon base, with an extension to the enclosure and a subsidiary enclosure to the east. The focus of revealed activity lay just against the south-east corner of the pylon base.

The northern area (Figures 3 and 7)
The north-west corner of the enclosure was formed by the junction of two gullies (521 and 638), both shallow 'U' shaped in profile. The eastern terminus of the W-E gully (638) was truncated by a later ditch (545, see phase 3). The N-S gully (521) was interrupted by the western edge of the pylon base, and continued southwards as gully 755 to a terminus approximately 19.4 m from the northern end. Subsequently the northern part of gully 521 was recut as ditch 525. The articulated skeleton of a small horse (524) was revealed in the lower sandy silt fill (523) of the ditch, its presence possibly accounting for the olive brown colour of 523. Two postholes (724 and 748 – see Fig. 9, Section 119), each with surviving postpipes, were located just to the east of the southern terminus of gully 755. Both measured

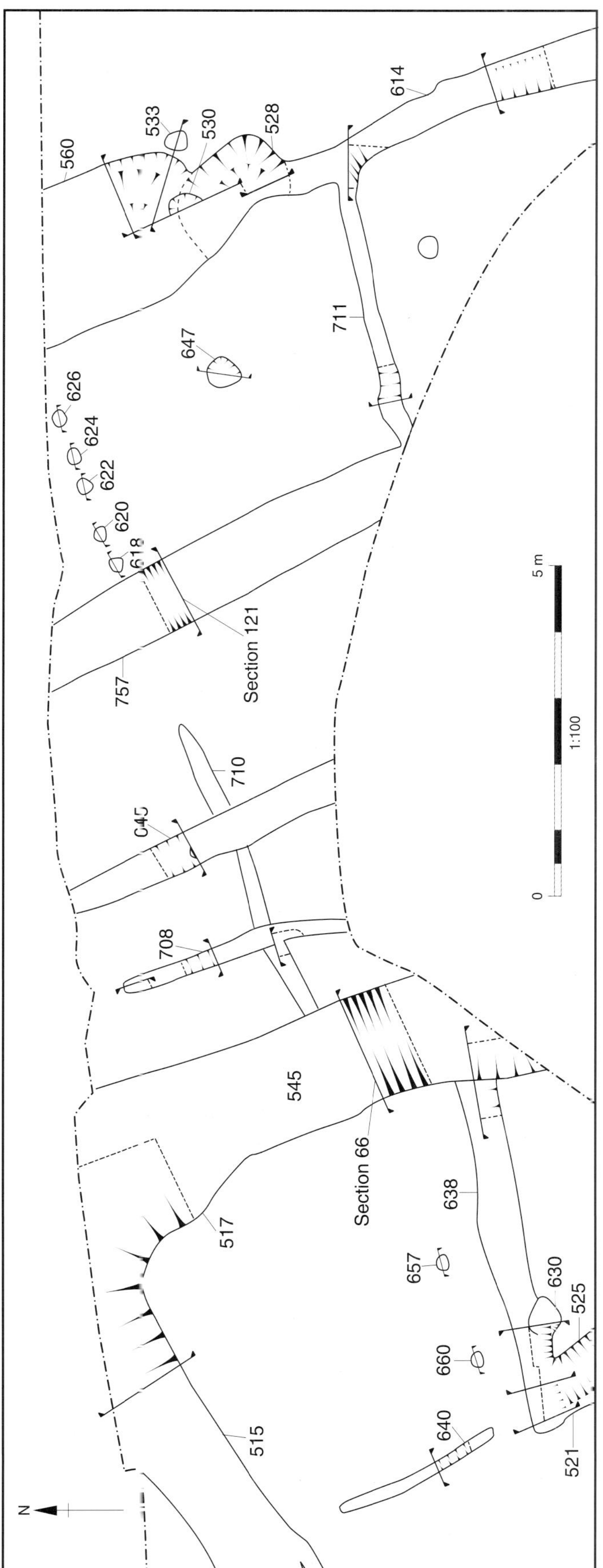

Figure 7: Detail plan of northern area

Figure 8: Detail plan of southern area

approximately 0.45 m in diameter × 0.15 m deep, with the postpipes suggesting that the original posts were between 0.16 m and 0.20 m in diameter.

Approximately 3.5 m to the west of gully 521, and parallel to it, was a poorly defined linear feature (777) approximately 26 m long. The southern terminus was excavated, revealing a bowl shaped gully 0.45 m deep, which produced a few pottery sherds from its sandy silt fill. At its mid-point an irregular linear feature ran eastwards under the pylon base. It is possible that this represents a continuation of gully 668 (see phase 1), although this was not investigated further.

Immediately west of feature 777 was a short curving gully cut by a large shallow sub-circular pit 670. A small pit (713), which may represent the terminus of the gully, was investigated along with 670. Both features contained sterile light grey fills of silty sand.

Apart from the horse skeleton, finds from the features in this part of the enclosure were restricted to a few late 11th – to late 12th-century pottery sherds and animal bone fragments from gullies 638 and 525, and from the terminus of feature 777.

The north-east corner of the enclosure was defined by a shallow 'V' shaped gully (711) extending to the east from under the pylon base. The gully appeared to be a continuation of gully 638. At a distance of 4 m from the pylon base, gully 711 turned southwards (recorded as gully 614) and continued south to a point against the east side of the pylon base (see Fig. 3), where it was truncated by disturbance caused by the base construction. Although the junction of 711 and 614 appeared to merge with pit 528 (see phase 1), no relationship was established. No finds were recovered from either gully.

A 'V' shaped ditch (645), which ran from the north baulk to the north edge of the pylon base, may be associated with this enclosure. It cut the phase 1 gully 710, and was of similar dimensions to enclosure ditch 638. Two pottery sherds were recovered from the upper fill (644).

The southern area (Figures 3, 6 and 8)
The south-east corner of the enclosure was defined by a series of linear features and recuts, extending ENE from the edge of the pylon base.

Evidence of a primary cut for the ENE ditch was seen in the steep-sided gully (816) close by the pylon base (see Fig. 8 and Fig. 9 Section 143), and the eastern terminus (734), revealed in section further to the east (see Fig. 6).

The primary gully appeared to be almost completely removed by a redefinition of the feature as ditch 578 (also recorded as 536 and 732), a steep-sided 'V' shaped cut averaging 1.30 m wide × 1.0 m deep, which at its eastern end cut the large phase 1 feature 539 (see Fig. 6 and Fig. 9 Section 98). There was some indication in the angle of the fill horizons of this cut that there may have been a bank on the southern side of the ditch (see Fig. 9 Section 75). Ditch 578/732 was itself truncated by another recut (587, see Fig. 6), which was slightly shallower and did not extend so far to the north-east. A short length of gully (704) was seen to cut the north side of ditch 578/732 close to the pylon base (Fig. 8).

The lower fills of ditch 578/732, where excavated, consisted mainly of light grey sandy silts, with few finds present in the sections excavated near the eastern terminus. However, upper fills of both 578 and 587 (537 and 538 respectively) produced sizeable assemblages of late 11th – to late 12th-century pottery and bone; in the section close to the pylon, where the ditch was recorded as 732, the upper fills again produced more pottery, in particular fill 700, which produced 25 sherds (see Fig. 8 Section 113).

The line of ditch 578/732 turned slightly more to the west as it ran under the pylon base. A complicated sequence of deposits were identified to the south (Fig. 8),

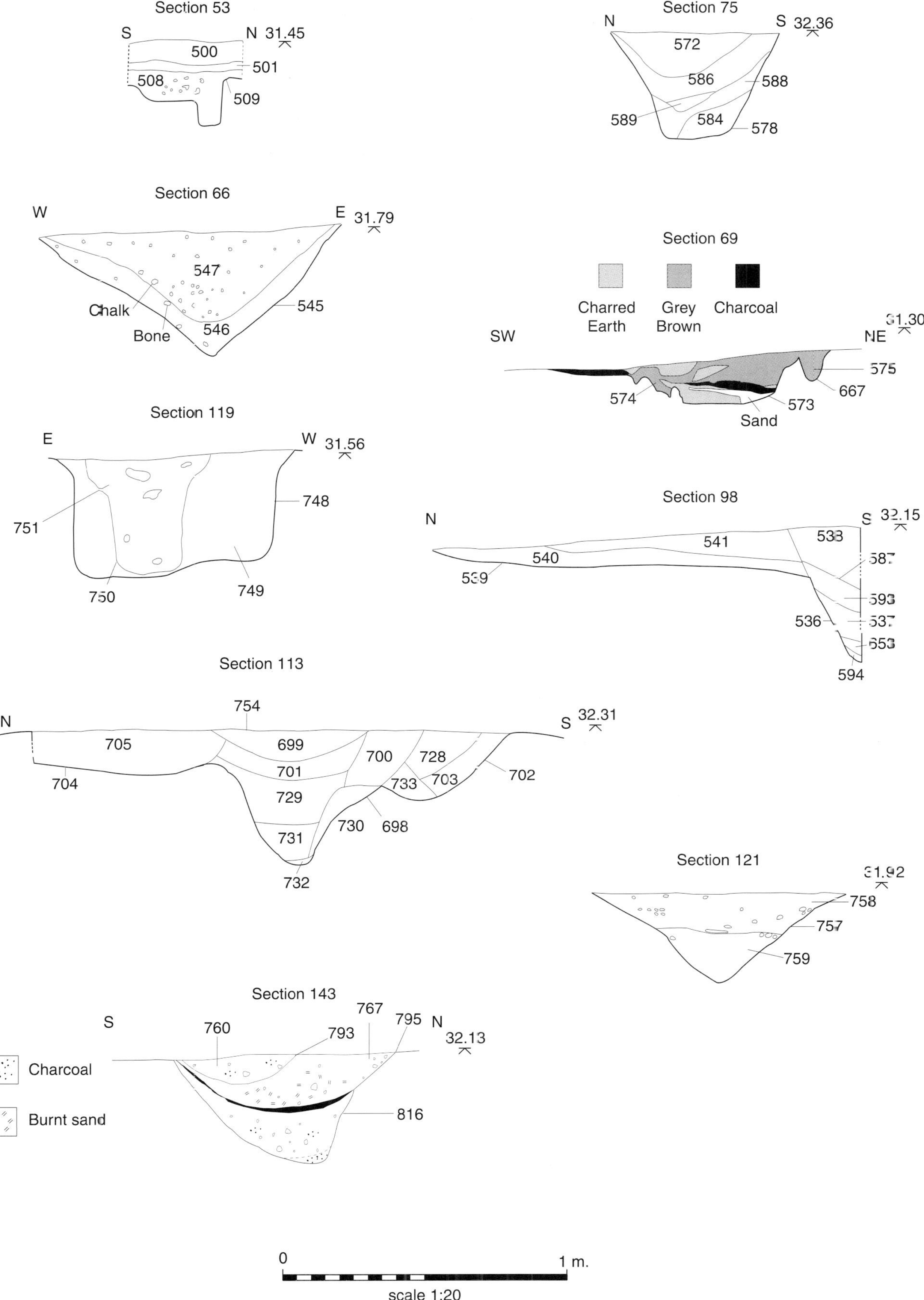

Figure 9: Sections

consisting of a shallow gully (793) filled with sandy silt dumped deposits containing a high proportion of charcoal and burnt clay, and some pottery. Gully 793 appeared to cross the line of a NS gully (652).

Gully 652 defined the west side of what was probably a second enclosure, in the south-east of the site. It turned eastwards immediately east of the pylon base, and ran for a further 19 m (recorded as gully 702) towards the east edge of excavation. The truncation of the southern end of gully 652 could imply that there was a return to the east at this point also, effectively forming a rectangular paddock. One linear feature was identified within the angle formed by gullies 652 and 702. Gully 814, which was shallow and 'U' shaped and devoid of finds, was approximately 6 m long and could possibly be seen as an extension of feature 793. The enclosure formed by 652/702 may have gone out of use before the end of phase 2 as the ditch appeared to be cut by both gully 793 and ditch 578/732.

Phase 3

Phase 3 (Figs. 3 and 4) is characterised by a later arrangement of rectilinear enclosure or field ditches that overlay and stratigraphically post-dated the features and gullies of phases 1 and 2. The principle elements of the ditch systems, from west to east, were represented by ditches 507 (south-west), 515, 787, 545, 757 and 838.

The ditches were in nearly all cases steep-sided and V shaped, and measured 1.5–2.0.m in width and between 0.90 m and 1.2 m deep. Representative sections are illustrated for ditches 545 and 757 (Fig. 9 Sections 66 and 121). It is likely that localised truncation by deeper ploughing was responsible for the apparent narrowing of the ditches in the north-west corner and the central-south parts of the site.

A small assemblage of pottery was found in the fills of the ditches close to the northern edge of the site, in particular deposits 516 and 518, fills of ditches 515 and 517 respectively (for ditch 517 see Fig. 7). Of possibly greater significance was the relatively large assemblage recovered from ditch 757 (14 sherds from the lower fill 759), which extended south-eastwards from the north baulk to the pylon base. The pottery from 759 may also be slightly later than that from the other features, being possibly mid 12th century in date. Away from the central-north part of the site, the ditch fills of this phase were notable for the absence of finds in the excavated sections.

Unphased features (Figures 3 and 4)

Two features were partially revealed against the northern baulk, a shallow 'L' shaped gully (785), and a part of a sub-circular pit (798). Both had grey silty-sand fills and produced no finds. The shape of the gully could suggest a structural function, although its orientation does not point to an obvious link with the activity to the south.

The junction of features 668 and 696 was disturbed by a shallow sub-rectangular pit (679) that produced a quantity of late medieval or early post-medieval tile fragments.

Later deposits

All features described above were overlain by a sandy silt ploughsoil (504) and a sandy loam topsoil (500). The only modern feature of note was a hardcore trackway surface (502, not illustrated) that extended from the west side of the pylon base to the south-west corner of the site. The construction of this (503) had slightly impacted upon the archaeological deposits in the south-west corner, but not to the extent that the interpretation of those features was compromised.

The preservation of deposits

The interpretation of the dating and duration of activity at the site must be subject to a degree of reservation concerning the extent of late and post-medieval disturbance and trunction. The results of the present archaeological works suggest that the excavated site was occupied for a relatively short period of time between the late 11th century and the middle of the 12th century. However, it is clear that occupation continued in the vicinity throughout the medieval and post-medieval period. Only a modest overburden of some 0.40 m was present over the site, and it remains possible that insubstantial or lightly founded structures or buildings of later date could have been severely truncated or conceivably destroyed altogether by later (post-medieval) ploughing. The subsoil of coarse gravel at the east end of the site would have required much less substantial footings for structures in comparison with the softer sand subsoil at the western end, so paradoxically the deposits or features situated over the firmer subsoil might be more easily truncated. Furthermore, the light sandy soil, and the slope of the site down to the south-west, would encourage erosion of the topsoil by the elements, once the surface was disturbed by ploughing.

Pre-medieval activity

Very little Romano-British material was recovered during the excavation, occurring as residual material in the ditch fills, and no features were dated to that period. This supports one of the conclusions drawn from the excavations in Springhead in 1994–5, that the Roman settlement was quite tightly confined to the road corridor of Watling Street (Boyle Early 1998).

The general development of the site in the medieval period

The documentary and excavated evidence shows that Wingfield Bank was the site of a medieval settlement, originally *Wenifalle*, which was established in the late 11th or early 12th century and persisted through the 13th and 14th centuries. Domestic occupation in the immediate area of the excavations seems to have ended by the middle of the 12th century, but the documentary sources show that the settlement persisted beyond this time. *Wenifalle* is first mentioned in written records in 1199, at which time it owed tithes to the Archbishop of Canterbury that were to be transferred to Rochester Priory. Thereafter references to *Wenifalle* occur throughout the 13th and 14th centuries. The size and nature of the medieval occupation is not known, but the site is in a classic location for secondary settlement. The place-name *Wenifalle* suggests a windy, exposed site, presumably due to its location on the crest of a high headland overlooking the Ebbsfleet Valley to the west.

The archaeological evidence suggests that the excavated area was substantially reorganised into large enclosures after the middle of the 12th century. The enclosures presumably represent part of the farmland of *Wenifalle*, with the focus of occupation further to the north. By the end of the 18th century, *Wenifalle* is represented on early maps and plans by a single, isolated farmstead 100 m to the north-east of the excavated area. Unfortunately, the limited scope of the excavation can shed no further light on the question of whether the settlement had always been a single farmstead, which shifted north-eastwards over time, or whether an originally larger settlement had shrunk to this size by the post-medieval period. It is also unclear whether occupation had been continuous on the site throughout the later medieval period, or whether the site had been abandoned and subsequently resettled. The farm site was redeveloped as a supermarket in recent times.

The medieval settlement

Phase 1

The excavations revealed only a limited area of the settlement, and its overall nature and extent remain unknown. The heavily truncated structural remains at the east edge of the site suggest a peasant dwelling of modest status, orientated NNW-SSE, probably of timber and earthen construction. No medieval roof tile was recovered from the site, suggesting that the building was roofed with thatch or wooden shingles. It appears to have been a two-roomed structure with an entrance at the mid-point of the west wall, and a partition. A chalky area and a spread of burnt patches suggest the remains of an open hearth within the northern half of the building. There was no evidence to clarify the function of the two rooms, although the presence of a hearth in the northern room points to domestic use. The building measured only 10 × 4 m internally, and the proposed entrance was only 1 m wide; this, combined with the lack of evidence for any form of drainage or stalling in the south room, suggests that the south room would not have been used for keeping livestock. It may simply have provided additional domestic accommodation. Alternatively, it may have served as a store-room for food or produce, and the very clearly defined posthole 604 could have supported a loft for additional storage space on the east side of the room.

Another possible building is suggested by the line of postholes close to the northern edge of the site, possibly defining the south wall of a building extending beyond the baulk. The rectilinear alignment of shallow gullies extending to the south-west and appearing to link up with the similar gullies extending north-east from the oven site could suggest that the structures were contemporary and associated.

The two large hollows, 539 and 560, were each situated close to these proposed buildings. In some respects both features could be said to display characteristics of the sunken-featured building (SFB) commonly found on settlements in the early and mid Saxon periods. Both were of a fairly uniform depth of approximately 0.30 m, and had reasonably level bases rising at a shallow angle to the surface of the subsoil. Manganese staining, sometimes an indicator of the presence of decayed organic matter, was evident in some of the lower fills of both features. However, with neither hollow was there any associated structural evidence in the form of postholes – either, as is typical, at the 'gable' ends, or in the form of subsidiary postholes around the sides, and there was no evidence in the finds assemblages for any activity of this date.

While late Saxon or post-Conquest buildings with sunken floors or cellars are not unusual in urban contexts (for example see Blair 1994, 161–4 and figs 93–4), known instances of sunken featured buildings dating to later than the 10th century in rural environments are currently still rare. Examples are known from Wharram Percy and Gomeldon (see Chapelot Fossier 1980, 207), but in both cases convincing evidence of the structural elements of the buildings was also present. A particularly striking example was excavated more recently at Stebbingford, Essex (Medlycott 1996, 121 and fig. 13), but here there was evidence for probable timber shuttering to retain the pit walls; a deliberately laid spread of gravel was present on the base of the pit, and crude steps or step supports of flint cobbles survived, leading down into the pit. There were also substantial assemblages of domestic finds. Most recently, excavations only 2 km to the south-east of the present site, in advance of the Channel Tunnel Rail Link at Northumberland Bottom, Gravesham, have located a small sunken-floored building set within a sub-rectangular ditched enclosure, which contained a possible corn-drying or malting oven (Glass 1999, 198–9). This complex is currently dated to the 12th to 14th centuries (URS 1999, 3 and fig. 7).

The Northfleet hollows lacked any form of additional structural evidence, and produced very few finds. The northern feature (560) produced some pottery, but all of it came from the north-west corner, suggesting that it derived from the possible building partly revealed in the northern group. The undisturbed fills of feature 539 produced no finds at all. It therefore seems unlikely that these hollows were either SFBs or cellars. It is more probable that they represent shallow quarries, dug for clay and sand material to make wall daub. It is probably no coincidence that both hollows were located close to the sites of buildings.

On the western edge of the site, the heavily burnt deposits in and around the irregular feature 573, and its close proximity to the semi-circular platform of chalk 554, clearly suggest a hearth or possibly an oven base. The beamslot to its south contained fragments of fired clay suggestive of wall daub, but the lack of a corresponding beamslot or other structural evidence to the north or east of the hearth and burnt area makes it difficult to postulate a building within which the hearth was set. The slot may have housed a windbreak. There was no evidence for any kind of craft or industrial activity taking place on the site, and it seems likely that this feature was essentially domestic or agricultural in function.

Phase 2

A second phase of activity is represented by the enclosure partially revealed around the perimeter of the pylon base. From the repeated deposition of burnt material, and the concentration of pottery, bone and oyster shells in the features against the south-east side of the pylon base, the focus of occupation, presumably one or more buildings, probably lay under the footprint of the pylon base itself. It is perhaps reasonable to suggest a dwelling surrounded by a modest enclosure, with an access way to the west and a paddock to the south-east.

Phase 3

The combined evidence of the stratigraphic sequence and phasing suggests that occupation of the site had ceased by the middle of the 12th century, and that the original, slightly haphazard arrangement of boundaries was superseded by a pattern of more substantial ditches. Allowing for variable truncation, their similar shape and size suggests a unified effort to redefine the existing land division, and in many instances these new ditches appear to replace existing boundaries; for instance this is seen in the way that ditch 838 cuts the terminus of ditch 652 – presumably 652 originally turned to the east to enclose the south-east area of the site. Similarly ditch 545 appears to follow a line originally denoted by the terminus of 710, and possibly by 638.

In almost all cases, the fills of the phase 3 ditches were uniform light brown sandy silts with very few finds, supporting the idea that the areas defined by the ditches were not occupied. The one exception to this is the fill of ditch 757, which yielded pottery perhaps dating to the mid 12th century, suggesting a continuation of domestic activity just beyond the north baulk.

Given the light and friable nature of the soil, the fact that the phase 3 ditches showed no evidence of being recut could be construed as evidence of still more shift (or shrinkage) of the settlement to the north, and the relatively rapid reversion of this area to open wasteland or pasture.

The nature of the medieval settlement

The settlement seems to have been agricultural in nature, with no evidence for any kind of specialised craft or industrial activity. The absence of Saxon settlement in the vicinity suggests that *Wenifalle* was a secondary settlement, probably established from Northfleet, during the later 11th century. The pottery and small finds assemblages are unexceptional, and consistent with what might be expected of a low to middling status rural settlement of the time.

The economic evidence suggests a mixed agricultural regime, with wheat, barley, oats and rye all represented in the charred plant assemblages (Pelling, below). Cereal processing waste and weeds are present, as well as cereal products, suggesting that the settlement was producing grain, as well as consuming it. Of particular interest is the presence of significant quantities of pulses, including broad bean, bean/vetch/pea and cultivated vetch, and weeds associated with cultivated garden crops of this kind. In her report on the charred plant remains, Ruth Pelling notes that the cultivation of legumes such as vetch seems to have formed an important component of the economy of Kent and may have been adopted at a particularly early date. The weeds present in the charred plant assemblages indicate a link with calcareous clay soils, suggesting that the settlement may have been involved in exploitation of the chalk downland to the south of the site, as well as the sandy, gravelly soils of the immediate area. The pastureland of Northfleet certainly extended up into the Downland valleys to the south (Everitt 1986, 85).

All the major domestic species were represented in the animal bone assemblage (Charles, below), but in insufficient quantities to provide much additional information about the agricultural regime of the settlement. Cattle, sheep, pigs and horses were present, with cattle probably being the most numerous. A single cattle mandible from a senile animal was identified, providing evidence that at least some of the animals were kept until they were very old; this supports the view that cattle were kept on site for traction and possibly for milk, as well as for meat.

The charred plant, animal, fish and bird bone evidence together suggests a varied diet, of a good standard. Most of the animal bone assemblage represents kitchen waste rather than butchery refuse, and Bethan Charles notes (see below) that not all beef bones had been stripped for meat and marrow. This may suggest a relatively comfortable standard of living. The lagomorph bones suggest that hare and/or rabbit were eaten; rabbit was a recent introduction to England at this period, and would have been an expensive food. Herring, cod, flatfish and oysters were eaten, and were presumably fairly readily available from ports on the Thames estuary a little way to the north of the site. A single galliform bone suggests that domestic fowl may also have been kept. In addition to cereals and pulses, the charred plant assemblages also provide evidence for the use of hazelnuts, juniper berry, and possibly sloe or plum.

Given the limitations of the archaeological evidence, it is not possible to be certain whether all this material derives from the excavated buildings and enclosures, or whether some of it may have spread from outside the excavated area. The structural evidence from the site suggests a peasant settlement of middling status, whose inhabitants might not be expected to have had access to expensive rabbit meat (except perhaps by poaching), or indeed to have discarded beef bones with meat and marrow still on them. It remains possible, therefore, that the excavated area lay on the periphery of a more prosperous establishment, which was not recovered in the investigations. Conversely, the apparent prosperity of the settlement may have more to do with its location on the north Kent coast, close to the Thames estuary and in the hinterland of London, in the richest, most fertile and most heavily settled area of the county. Pottery types present on the site were also common in London at this period, and trade must have been commonplace. Both as consumers and as producers, the inhabitants may have benefited from the river and the city, and enjoyed a considerably higher standard of living than their contemporaries elsewhere in the country.

The site in its regional context

Until recently, very little archaeological information was available for medieval rural settlement of this date and type in Kent. However, recent excavations in advance of development have located a number of sites that appear to follow a broadly similar pattern.

Recent excavations in advance of the Channel Tunnel Rail Link at Northumberland Bottom, south of Gravesend and some 2 km south-east of the present site, have identified a medieval occupation site dated provisionally to 1050–1150, occupying a shallow terrace near the foot of a hill (Glass 1999, 198–9; URS 1999, 3–4 and Figs. 4 and 7). The provisional interpretation of the evidence suggests one or more timber structures with associated pits and a boundary ditch. A circular ditched enclosure near the crest of the hill appears to have functioned as a livestock enclosure, and is considered to be of the same date (ibid.). The enclosure was replaced at some point between the late 12th and 14th centuries by a sub-rectangular ditched enclosure which contained evidence of occupation including a small, sunken-floored building containing a possible corn-drying or malting oven.

Further excavations at the opposite end of the Channel Tunnel Rail Link at Westenhanger Castle, Westenhanger, have identified a concentration of features of similar date (Glass 1999, 219–20) that have been provisionally identified as the remains of a medieval farmstead established in the late 11th century (URS 2000 *passim*). At least three rectangular timber structures have now been recognised, separated by enclosure ditches, with rubbish pits nearby. As at the present site, the evidence suggests that the Westenhanger farmstead was substantially reorganised in the later 12th or early 13th century, when a new ditch and enclosure system was laid out associated with pits and possible animal pens. There did not appear to be any buildings associated with this later phase of occupation on the site, and it is suggested that, as at the present site, the focus of occupation may have shifted to the north (ibid.).

Recent excavations at Monkton, Thanet have identified four early medieval buildings and several related features, mostly lying within a series of ditched enclosures (Pratt et al. forthcoming, 301–4, 319–22). Pottery dating suggests that occupation began on the site in the late 11th or early 12th century, and that the site had perhaps been abandoned by the late 12th century (ibid. 308), with the main focus of occupation possibly shifting elsewhere. The Monkton buildings were better preserved than those at the present site, and some were more elaborate in layout and construction, but they share similarities in the use of beamslot and posthole construction techniques, and in the division of the interior space into different rooms by the use of cross passages and screens.

The most striking point of comparison between the four sites, however, is their remarkably similar chronology and sequence of development, particularly given their wide dispersal through the county. All four sites represent farmsteads or small settlements that were apparently established on 'new' land, in the later 11th or early 12th century; none of the sites seems to have been occupied during the Anglo-Saxon period. At each site, the buildings seem to have been abandoned during the later part of the 12th century. At Northfleet and Westenhanger the landscape was subject to considerable reorganisation, with the digging of substantial new enclosure ditches, and the focus of occupation seems to have shifted elsewhere.

This suggests an interesting line for future research. The results discussed above suggest that there may have been a comparatively early move outwards from primary settlements in Kent during the late 11th and early 12th centuries, with secondary settlements reoccupying poorer land that had been abandoned in the Anglo-Saxon period. The results also suggest the possibility of significant settlement shift in the late 12th century, and further excavation and research would be necessary to establish whether this is a general pattern or a localised or irregular phenomenon. The present sites can unfortunately shed no light on the interesting question of whether the abandoned settlements shifted elsewhere, but carried on much as before, or whether they were replaced by more substantial holdings. In this respect, research in the vicinity of moated sites may be particularly rewarding

Artefactual evidence

Roman pottery
by Paul Booth

Medieval pottery
by Paul Blinkhorn

Only three Roman pottery sherds were recovered, all of which were from later contexts. These were fragments of Central Gaulish samian ware, Oxford colour-coated ware and a local sandy reduced coarse ware. All presumably derived from the nearby Roman settlement of Springhead and none requires further comment.

Introduction

The medieval pottery assemblage comprised 293 sherds with a total weight of 4543 g. The minimum number of vessels, by measurement of rim sherd length, was 1.76. The pottery occurrence by number and weight of sherds per context by fabric type is shown in Table 1.

Table 1: Pottery occurrence by number and weight (in g) of sherds per context by fabric type

	F1		F2		F3		F4		F5		F6		
Context	No	Wt	No	Wt	No	Wt	No	Wt	No	Wt	No	Wt	Date
513	2	32			4	57							L11thC?
516			2	8									L11thC
518			2	11									L11thC
520	1	22	2	36									L11thC?
522	3	24	1	16									L11thC
535	1	335											L11thC
537	42	642	2	15	2	21							L11thC?
538	40	631	6	75	5	27							L11thC?
546	1	4	3	40	1	7							L11thC
547			3	10									L11thC
549	2	28											L11thC?
551	2	17											L11thC?
555	1	7											L11thC?
557	2	24											L11thC?
572	5	44											L11thC?
577	1	2											L11thC?
584	1	7											L11thC?
585	1	18											L11thC?
588	1	5											L11thC?
605			2	17									L11thC
629					1	6							L11thC
631			1	14									L11thC?
644	2	20											L11thC?
649	1	10	1	4									L11thC?
651	1	14	7	112									L11thC?
655	6	38											L11thC?
656	5	64	4	72	1	1			1	50			L11thC?
664	2	8	1	7									L11thC
671			1	6									L11thC
672	1	4											L11thC?
678	1	1											L11thC?
682	1	35	1	38									L11thC?
692					6	105							L11thC?
700	17	284	7	178	1	10							L11thC?
701	1	2					1	77					M12thC?

(continued)

Context	F1		F2		F3		F4		F5		F6		Date
	No	Wt	No	Wt	No	Wt	No	Wt	No	Wt	No	Wt	
703	1	5	1	5									L11thC?
705	1	6	1	6									L11thC?
716	1	35											L11thC?
735	1	93											L11thC?
739	2	58	1	47									L11thC?
743	11	57											L11thC?
747	1	95											L11thC?
756	1	21											L11thC
759	14	99	1	18							1	11	M12thC?
760			4	154									L11thC
766	1	19											L11thC?
767	1	9	1	8									L11thC?
769	3	50											L11thC?
770	14	119											L11thC
773			2	30									L11thC
777	1	6											L11thC
802			1	26									L11thC?
815	5	31	1	4	1	6							L11thC?
818	1	4	1	23	1	63							L11thC?
848	4	58	2	7									L11thC
849	2	35											L11thC
858	1	33											L11thC?
860	1	1											L11thC?
	211	3156	62	987	23	303	1	77	1	50	1	11	

The majority of the context-specific assemblages are datable to the later 11th or early 12th century, and largely comprise undecorated coarseware jars. Single fragments from two glazed jugs were also present, and probably date to the early to mid 12th century. The wares are all types which are well known in Kent and the City of London, although the assemblage is one of the very few of this date to have been excavated in the area in recent years.

Fabrics

Some of the pottery types are common in London, and, where appropriate, the Museum of London fabric codes have been used (Vince 1985, 38). Such wares are also known from other sites in Kent, particularly from excavations at nearby Dartford (Mynard 1973) and also Eynsford Castle (Rigold Fleming 1973). Consequently, they have also been referenced to those sites where possible.

Fabric 1: Shelly Limestone Ware (MoLAS code: SHEL). Equivalent to the 'Shell-gritted wares' from Eynsford Castle (Rigold Fleming 1973, 106–7). Dated in London to the late 11th – late 12th century. At Rochester, shelly wares were noted beneath pre-1087/9 levels, whilst at Eynsford Castle, similar material dominated the pottery assemblage from the late 11th century (McCarthy Brooks 1988, 184). All the Northfleet vessels were undecorated apart from thumbed rims (Fig. 10, NP1) and a single bodysherd with a fragment of an incised wavy line. 205 sherds, 3.115 g, MNV = 1.35.

Fabric 2: Early Medieval Sand and Shell Ware (EMSS). Equivalent to the 'Sandy – shelly' fabric from Dartford (Mynard 1973, 188). Dated in London to early 11th-late 12th century. 62 sherds, 987 g, MNV = 0.41.

Fabric 3: Reduced Sandy Ware. Grey fabric with dark to light grey surfaces. Moderate to dense sub-rounded quartz up to 0.5 mm, rare black ironstone and shell fragments, the latter up to 1 mm. Some vessels show evidence of knife-trimming on the outer lower body, and sherds from two vessels with vertical applied strips were noted (Fig. 10, NP5). Equivalent to the 'sand-tempered' fabric from Dartford, given the code 'ST *b*' at Eynsford (Mynard 1973, 189). Appears contemporary with fabrics 1 and 2 at this site. 23 sherds, 303 g, MNV = 0.

Fabric 4: Coarse London Ware (LCOAR). Sandy glazed ware (Vince 1985). Single fragment of a slashed rod handle (Fig. 10, NP6). 1 sherd, 77 g, MNV = 0.

Fabric 5: Oxidized Sandy Ware. Possibly an oxidized version of fabric 3? Very similar fabric and appears to be contemporary. The single sherd is an unusual tubular spout from a pitcher with applied strips (Fig. 10, NP7). 1 sherd, 50 g, MNV = 0.

Fabric 6. London Ware (LOND). Sandy glazed ware (Vince 1985). Single sherd from a green-glazed pitcher with incised line and applied slip decoration (Fig. 10, NP8). 1 sherd, 11 g, MNV = 0.

Illustrations (Figure 10)

NP1: Context 537, fabric F1. Rimsherd from large jar. Grey fabric with brick-red surfaces.

NP2: Context 700, fabric F1. Rimsherd from large jar. Grey fabric with brick-red surfaces. Light sooting on the rim-bead.

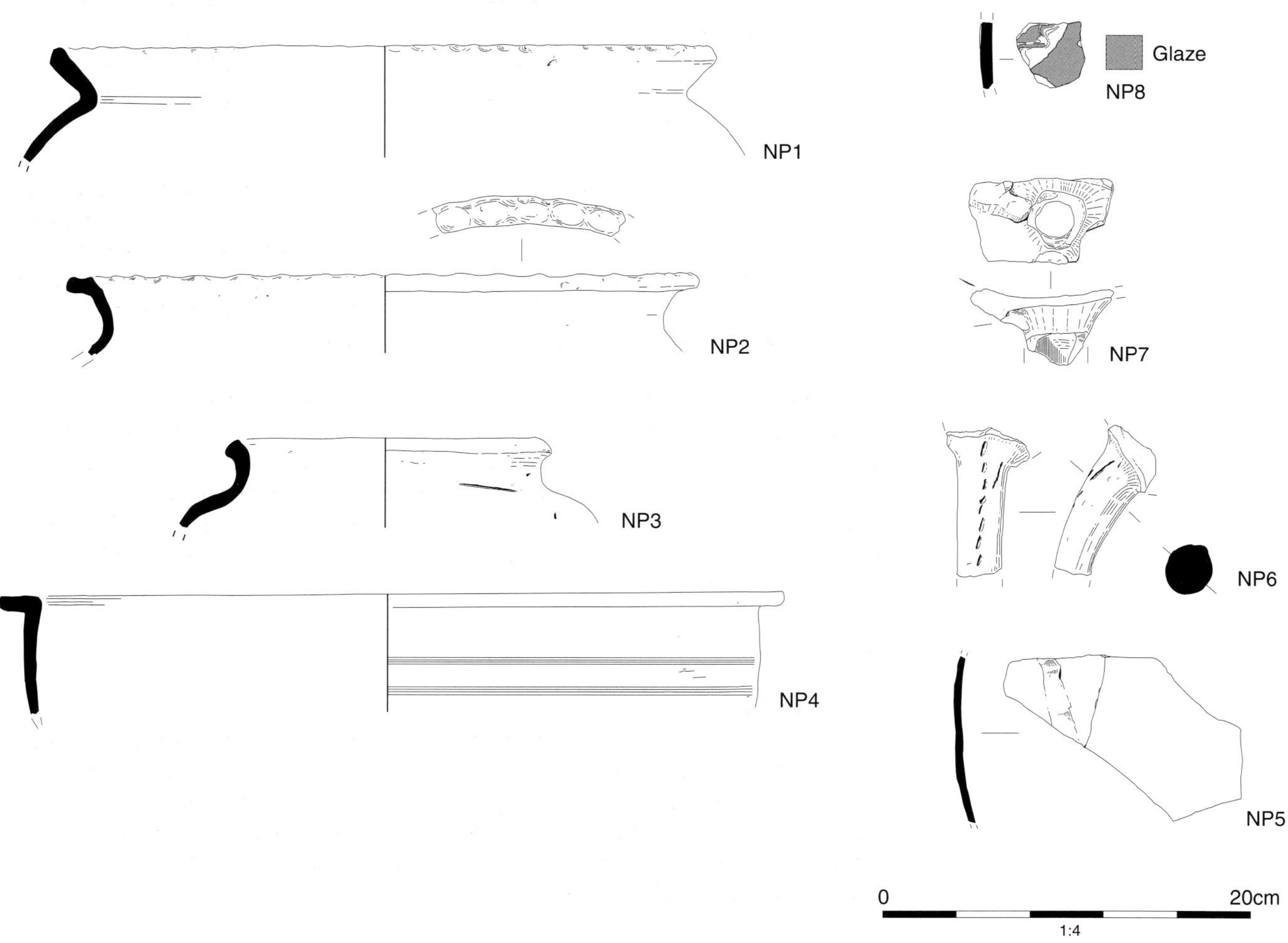

Figure 10: Pottery

NP3: Context 739, fabric F2. Rimsherd from jar. Grey fabric with variegated orange and pale grey surfaces.

NP4: Context 760, fabric F2. Rimsherd from bowl. Grey fabric with purplish-black surfaces.

NP5: Context 818, fabric F3. Bodysherd with applied strip. Grey fabric with darker surfaces.

NP6: Context 701, fabric F4. Rod handle from jug. Grey fabric with orange surfaces. Numerous spots of decayed, under-fired glaze.

NP7: Context 656, fabric F5. Tubular spout from pitcher. Grey fabric with orange surfaces.

NP8: Context 759, fabric F6. Grey fabric with orange margins. Glossy green exterior glaze. White sgraffito slip decoration, appearing yellow under the glaze.

Chronology

The medieval pottery assemblage indicates that there was a brief period of occupation during the 11th-early 12th century. The vast majority of the context-specific assemblages did not contain any glazed wares, and only two sherds of such pottery were noted at the entire site. The make-up of the assemblage has the same broad characteristics as those from London from the 11th-12th century (Vince 1985, Fig. 7), i.e. purely unglazed wares during the 11th century with small quantities of glazed wares first appearing during the early to mid 12th century. It is worthy of note, however, that SHEL is far more common at this site than in contemporary assemblages from London, which, when given the widespread occurrence of such wares in Kent (e.g. McCarthy Brooks 1988, 183), suggests that it was probably made at one or more Kentish sources. Conversely, EMSS is far more common in London, suggesting that it was not manufactured in Kent.

In theory, it is possible to divide the early medieval assemblages from th s site into two phases, i.e. early 11th century (contexts producing only EMSS) and later 11th century (contexts producing SHEL). However, all the assemblages which comprise only EMSS are very small, and consist of a handful of sherds, suggesting that there is no real difference in the dating of the two wares from this site, and that occupation did not begin until the final quarter of the 11th century.

The presence of only two sherds of glazed pottery indicates that activity at the site had all but ceased by the middle of the 12th century. The two sherds are both glazed London wares (LOND and LCOAR), and have been previously noted in Kent, at sites that are more distant from the City than Northfleet, such as Canterbury and Pivington Manor, Pluckley (Pearce et al. 1985, figs anc 21. Their low representation here would thus appear to be due to chronological rather than trade or functional considerations.

Fragmentation Analysis

The overall mean sherd weight for the assemblage is 15.5 g, which is reasonably good considering the friable nature of the shelly coarsewares, and the fact that the SHEL fabric is not as dense as the others. It was not possible to reconstruct any whole vessels, indicating that all the pottery is a product of secondary deposition, but the material does not seem to have been subject to much transportation and disturbance. The mean rimsherd size was 6.8% complete, which is again not unusual for pottery of this type.

Cross-fits

The somewhat homogeneous nature of the majority of the pottery from this site meant that the cross-fit analysis had to be limited mainly to rimsherds. Only one cross-fit was achieved, between contexts 537 and 538 (fills of phase 2 enclosure ditch 578 and its recut 587 respectively), with many joins from the base and lower body from a SHEL jar. This paucity would indicate that most of the deposits are the results of discrete actions, or came from different sources.

Vessel Analysis

The only vessels that were represented by rimsherds were in fabrics 1 and 2, and all were jars with the exception of a single bowl sherd. Pitchers were represented by the two sherds of London-type wares and the spout in fabric 5. Jugs in EMSS were present at Dartford (Mynard 1973, 188), but none were noted here, suggesting that the introduction of such vessels may post-date the early 12th century. Certainly, the Dartford group appears to date to the 13th century at the earliest (ibid. 187). This again suggests a different chronology for the use of the ware, as in London it had generally fallen from use by the end of the 12th century (Vince 1985, fig. 7). Jugs in this fabric were similarly rare at Eynsford Castle, and are also known from London, although jugs in SHEL ware are unknown in the city (ibid. 37).

There is good evidence to indicate that the rim diameter of a vessel is a reasonable representation of the capacity of the pot when it was complete (Blinkhorn in prep.). The SHEL and EMSS jar rims at this site appear mainly to derive from large vessels, which is confirmed by the fact that the mean rim diameter is 281.6 mm, with a standard deviation of 33 mm. Plotting the rim diameter of the Northfleet assemblage by MNV per diameter class (Table 2) confirms this. Large vessels in these fabrics are not uncommon (Rigold Fleming 1973, figs 11–14; Vince 1985, 37), and thus the presence of the large jars at this site is not likely to be an indication of an unusual or specialised function, but is simply a reflection of the apparently standard range of forms of the pottery types.

Table 2: Jar rim occurrence by MNV per diameter class

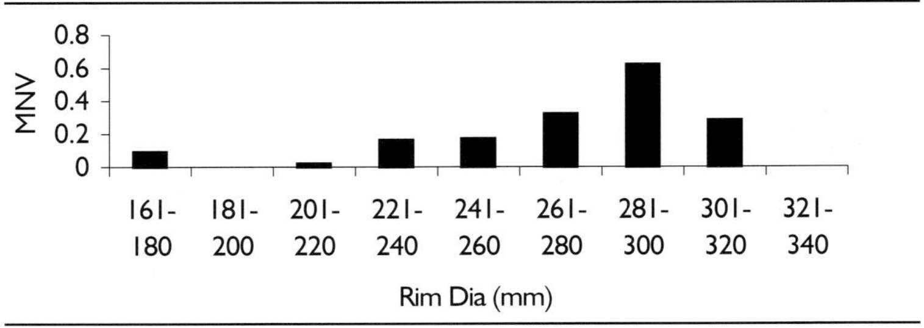

Ceramic building material and fired clay
by Kate Atherton

Introduction and methodology

The excavation produced an assemblage of 28 fragments of ceramic building material of a total weight of 2975 g, of which 21 were Romano-British and the remaining 7 were late medieval or early post-medieval. In addition, 633 g of fired clay was recovered from ten contexts and this is discussed at the end of the report.

Romano-British ceramic building material

Among the 21 fragments, only 11 were identifiable by type; 3 fragments were identified as from *tegulae* (flat roof tiles), 1 fragment as from an *imbrex*, and 7 from flat tiles.

The assemblage was recovered from features dating to the 11th and 12th centuries and so is considered residual. Too little material was found to postulate a Roman building in the immediate vicinity, and the material presumably derives from the small town at Springhead, nearby to the south-west.

Post-Roman ceramic building material

Seven fragments of roofing tile were identified as post-Roman and are probably late medieval or early post-medieval. Two of the fragments were found in context 680 and the remaining pieces were from context 689, both fills of probable post-medieval pits (679 and 688 respectively).

Fired clay

Ten contexts produced fragmentary pieces of fired clay with a total weight of 633 g (Table 3).

Table 3: Fired clay

Context	Weight (g)	Phase
508	232	1
513	95	1
523	1	2
549	67	1
610	51	1
651	88	2
672	1	2
682	3	1
760	69	2
762	26	1
Total	633	

One fragment, from context 508 (the fill of beamslot 509) had the remains of a small groove 12 mm wide, probably the impression of a wattle. This, in addition to the fact that several of the pieces had a smoothed surface, suggests that the fired clay was probably daub and had a structural function.

Flint and worked stone
by Philippa Bradley

A small assemblage of 31 pieces of worked flint, 20 pieces of burnt flint, 10 pieces of Niedermendig lava and 4 pieces of burnt unworked stone was recovered from the excavation. The majority of the material came from contexts that also produced 11th – to 12th-century pottery. The flint assemblage consists entirely of debitage, and most of it is fresh. It therefore seems likely that the majority of this material is associated with the medieval occupation. In addition 20 pieces of burnt unworked flint cobbles were recovered, many from the fill of feature 560, and possibly represent a dumped hearth. The 10 pieces of Niedermendig lava were recovered from the ploughsoil close to the northern edge of the site both in the evaluation (cxt 301) and the excavation (cxt 505). They are likely to have derived from quern material, and while it is possible that they are Roman in origin, the occurrence of Niedermendig lava querns in late Saxon and early medieval contexts is not unusual. Given the relative lack of residual Roman material on the site, a medieval provenance for this material is more likely.

Metalwork
by Leigh Allen

There were 16 metal objects recovered from the excavation; 7 are copper alloy and the remaining 9 are iron. The copper alloy objects are all fragments of thin metal sheet. The single fragment from context 760 is roughly rectangular with a slight raised ridge running along one edge. The 6 fragments from context 551 join up to form a long trapezoidal shaped strip with 2 small perforations at one end, one in each corner. The strip tapers very gradually along its length and has two slight raised ridges across the width towards each end. It is possible that this strip is a scale from a scale tang knife.

From context 700 there are two robust fragments of iron (SF 2 and 3) from the tips of horseshoes. They are curved along their length and they both have the remains of a single perforation through them; SF 2 has a corroded nail still *in situ*. Three short nails are probably horseshoe nails: SF 7 from context 557 and 2 further examples from contexts 537 and 762. All have short shanks and rectangular heads that are the same width as the shank. SF 4 from context 656 is an iron strip with a rectangular section that expands widthways along its length; it is broken and there is a square perforation with a nail or rivet still *in situ* on the break. The opposing end of the strip terminates in a square sectioned loop. This is possibly a handle from a vessel. The remaining two fragments are a nail shank with the head missing from context 747, and an irregularly shaped fragment of iron sheet with a square perforation through it from context 547.

Overall, the assemblage was small and unremarkable in the context of the site, and all the objects were in a very fragmentary and highly corroded condition. None of the objects can be seen as diagnostically significant. A complete catalogue is available in the project archive.

Ecofactual evidence

Animal bone
by Bethan Charles

Introduction and quantification

A total of 1556 fragments of bone were retrieved by hand from the site, although a large number of the bones were re-assembled, reducing the total to 764. From this number 54% were identified by element and species. Among the assemblage were the articulated and partially articulated skeletons of two horses and a partially articulated skeleton of a neo-natal piglet. All the bones that were related to each of the skeletons were counted as one, reducing the final total of identified bones to 175, as shown in Table 4.

Table 4: Number of hand-collected bones from site

Period	Cattle	Sheep	Horse	Pig	Dog	Rabbit	Frog	Fish	Unidentified	Total
Medieval	91	24	11	27	8	11	1	2	352	527

In addition to the hand collected material a number of bones were collected from the environmental samples, sieved through meshes of >10 *mm* and 10–4 mm where necessary (Table 6). The majority of this assemblage consisted of fish and minor mammal bones (see Ingrem below) as well as a few elements from cattle, sheep, pig and horse.

Methodology

The Minimum Number of Individuals (MNI) was calculated for the main domestic species from the most numerous elements from each individual species (Table 5).

Table 5: MNI for the main domestic species

Period	Sheep	Cattle	Pig	Horse
Medieval	3	7	3	2

Table 6: Number of sieved bones from environmental samples

Period	Cattle	Sheep	Horse	Pig	Unidentified	Total
Medieval	2	8	1	3	140	154

The caprine bones were surveyed, using the criteria of Boessneck (1969), and Prummel and Frisch (1986) in addition to the reference material housed at the OAU, to distinguish between sheep and goat bones. No goat bones were identified in the assemblage, so all caprine bones will be referred to as sheep in the text.

Ageing was based on tooth eruption and wear and epiphyseal fusion, although it is acknowledged that the latter is less reliable. Tooth eruption and wear was measured using a combination of Payne's (1973), Grant's (1982) and Halstead's (1985) tables for cattle and sheep. The timing of epiphyseal closure for cattle, sheep, pig and horse was measured against Silvers' (1969) tables and their adaptation by O'Connor (1982). Only the tables for the cattle bones have been included in the report since the other species were insufficiently represented in the assemblage to make the tables meaningful. Measurements were taken following von den Driesch (1979). All bone recording data is included in the archive.

Condition of bone

Over 50% of the bones in the assemblage had severe attritional damage in the form of flaking and pitting, characteristic of chemical etching. A small number of bones including a few fragments from the articulated skeleton in context 524 also had signs of root damage. As a result of this many of the bones were quite fragile and over 70% of the bones had fresh breaks. Very few of the elements identified had clear butchery marks and it s most likely that the attritional damage as well as the fresh breaks on the bones will have affected the identification of these marks.

A small number of the bones in the assemblage had tooth marks. Most were probably made by dogs and this may have affected the spatial distribution of many of the bones on the site. Additionally, one fragment from context 744 (a fill of gully 823) had signs of rodent gnaw marks. None of the fragments in the assemblage had been burnt.

Species representation

Table 4 shows the total number of bones collected from the site after fragment assembly. Over 50% of the bones identified were from cattle. The next most prevalent species were pigs and sheep. The MNI calculation supports the view that cattle were the most numerous animals found at the site. However, the bone material retrieved from environmental samples (Table 6) produced a higher relative proportion of sheep bone. This apparent anomaly could relate to the disposal patterns of bone waste for the different species.

Many of the cattle bones were complete which indicates that not all the meat and marrow from the cattle carcasses was being extracted. This may indicate a site of relatively high status.

Table 7 shows that none of the cattle were slaughtered before 2 to 3 years of age, with the majority killed at 3.5 to 4 years. A single cattle mandible was from a senile animal (Halstead 1985) indicating that at least some of the animals were kept until they were very old.

The rate of epiphyseal fusion in the sheep bones appears to indicate a variety in age at death. However, there were not enough indicative elements to enable more detailed information to be extracted. A single mandible was from an individual of 3–4 years of age. Sheep would have been kept primarily for their wool, milk and dung during this period.

The majority of the pigs from the site were young individuals under two years of age. At least two of the animals were male. A partial skeleton of a neo-ratal pig was found in context 690, the upper fill of late medieval or early post-medieval pit 688. This is a possible indicator of pig breeding, presumably related to the later activity at nearby Wingfield Bank farm.

Table 7: Epiphyseal fusion in cattle bones following Silver and adapted by O'Connor

Age	Element	Medieval	
		F	UF
9–18 mths	Humerus D	4	0
	Radius P	10	0
2–3 yrs	Metacarpal D	1	0
	Tibia D	0	3
	Metatarsal D	1	0
3.5–4 yrs	Humerus P	2	1
	Radius D	5	1
	Femur P	0	4
	Femur D	3	5
	Tibia P	0	3

Much of the horse bone assemblage came from the articulated skeleton in context 524 (the fill of recut phase 2 enclosure ditch 525). The majority of this skeleton was present including the skull, vertebrae, ribs and the back legs. The forelegs and scapulae were missing. The rate of epiphyseal fusion in the surviving elements indicates that the animal was 3–3.5 years of age at death. There was no indication as to the cause of death and it is possible that the animal may have become ill and died, leaving no trace on the bones. The horse was male and small to medium in stature (measurements from the bones can be seen in Table 8).

Table 8: Measurements of bones from articulated horse skeleton (524)

Element	Measurement	mm	Mean	Number
Metatarsal	GL	261–262	261.5	2
	Bd	42.8–43.4	43.1	2
Tibia	GL	332–336	334	2
	Bd	68.5	68.5	1

Only one other horse bone was complete enough for measurements (metatarsal from context 758 GL = 220 mm Bd = 46 mm).

The other partially articulated remains of a horse were found in context 782 (a lower fill of phase 3 field boundary ditch 781) and comprised a number of ribs and the sacrum, all the lumbar vertebrae and four of the thoracic vertebrae. Two of the thoracic vertebrae had signs of bone remodelling characteristic of osteoarthritis. This may indicate that the horse was old or that the animal may have been subjected to excessive strain.

One other fragment of unarticulated horse bone from context 758 (an upper fill of phase 3 ditch 757) also had signs of pathology. A complete metacarpal was found with metatarsal IV fused to the main bone along with a large amount of bone formation around the proximal articulation. It is likely that this may have been due to trauma.

There were a number of rabbit bones amongst the assemblage (from contexts 547, 549, 690 and 851). It is thought that rabbits may have been introduced from southern France or Spain during the late 11th and early 12th century (Veale 1957), and would have been a very expensive food source in this period.

A few fragments of dog bone were found in contexts concentrated in the eastern half of the site. Apart from part of a mandible, most of the bones were in poor condition, varied in size, and probably represent different individuals, but none of the elements were complete enough for meaningful measurement.

Discussion

Cattle appear to have been the most numerous animals kept at the site which may be typical of early medieval animal husbandry in the area. It is possible that the cattle were kept for traction purposes or that they provided milk as well as providing the bulk of the meat eaten by the inhabitants. The sheep would also have been kept for their secondary products such as wool, milk and dung, and not bred solely for their meat. Pigs, on the other hand, provide little in the way of secondary products and were almost certainly kept for their meat only.

Documentary evidence, such as the Domesday survey, points to the dominance of sheep in animal husbandry from the early medieval period (Trow-Smith 1957). However, results from urban medieval sites such as Exeter (Maltby 1979) and Flaxengate, Lincoln (O'Connor 1982) indicate that the occurrence of sheep bones on archaeological sites does not increase substantially relative to cattle and pig until after the 13th century. It appears that the remains from this site support that contention.

The majority of the assemblage appears to be kitchen waste since there were no concentrations of bone resembling butchery waste on the site. A few of the bones were partially complete which may indicate, as mentioned earlier, that not all of the beef carcasses were being stripped for meat and marrow. In addition to this the rabbit bones and fish bone indicate that the diet was slightly varied and may represent waste from a mid- to high-status site.

Small mammal, bird and fish remains
by Claire Ingrem

A small quantity of small mammal, amphibian, bird and fish remains was recovered from sieved environmental samples taken from a variety of features dating to the late 11th to late 12th centuries.

Methodology

The animal bones were identified and recorded at the Centre for Human Ecology and Environment (CHEE), Department of Archaeology, University of Southampton. All fragments were identified to species where possible with the exception of ribs and vertebrae, which were assigned to size categories. The completeness of the small mammal and bird bones was recorded using the zonal method developed by Serjeantson (1996). The incidence of surface modifications such as butchery, gnawing and burning was also noted. The size of fish was visually categorised with the aid of reference specimens as very small (< 150 mm), small (150–300 mm), medium (300–600 mm), large (600–1200 mm) and very large (1200–c 2000 mm). Frog and toad have been distinguished using the morphology of the pelvis.

Data

A total of 210 fragments of small mammal, bird and fish was retrieved from the samples (Tables 9 and 10), of which 29 could be identified to species or family. The most numerous species was fish although most of these fragments were unidentifiable spines, fin rays and miscellaneous fragments; for clarity these have been omitted from Table 11. The majority of fragments came from phases 1 and 2, with a smaller amount from phase 3.

Phases 1 and 2
Herring (*Clupea harengus*) is the only species identified, although lagomorph (rabbit or hare), rodent, amphibian, galliform (probably domestic fowl), gadidae (cod-family) and flatfish were also present (Table 9).

The beam slot and heavily burnt area produced 4 identifiable fragments: two belonging to lagomorph, a lumbar vertebra and 3rd phalanx, a rodent tibia and an

   THE EXCAVATION OF A MEDIEVAL RURAL SETTLEMENT AT NORTHFLEET, KENT

Table 9: Species representation of small mammal bird and fish in Phases 1 and 2

	Mesh size			Total
	>10	10–4	4–2	
Lagomorph		2		2
Rodent		4	1	5
Small mammal indet.		1		1
Amphibian indet.		4	1	5
Galliform		1		1
Bird indet.		1		1
Herring		3	5	8
Large gadid	3	3		6
Flatfish		3		3
Fish indet.	1	113	18	132
Unidentifiable		3	5	8
Total	4	138	30	172

Table 10: Species representation of small mammal, bird and fish in Phase 3

	Mesh size		Total
	10–4	4–2	
Toad	1		1
Amphibian indet.	9	3	12
Herring		3	3
Fish indet.		18	18
Unidentifiable	2	2	4
Total	12	26	38

Table 11: Species representation according to phase and feature (excluding unidentifiable and indeterminate fish)

	Phase 1 and 2			Phase 3	
	Beam slot/ Burnt area	Hearth/ dump material	Posthole line	Gully	Total
Lagomorph	2				2
Rodent	1	1	3		5
Small mammal indet.	1				1
Toad				1	1
Amphibian indet.		1	4	12	17
Galliform		1			1
Bird indet.		1			1
Herring		5	3	3	11
Large gadid		6			6
Flatfish		3			3
Total	4	18	10	16	48

unidentified small mammal rib fragment. The lagomorph vertebra, although of a similar size to rabbit, is unfused and may therefore belong to an immature hare.

Eighteen identifiable fragments (excluding indeterminate fish) came from the hearth and dump material; most were fish bones with herring, large gadid and flatfish all represented. The majority of fish bones were vertebra but an articular belonging to herring and the cleithra belonging to a large gadid (probably cod) were also present. In addition, a rodent femur, an amphibian vertebra, fragments of carpometacarpal and tarsometatarsus belonging to galliform were recovered. Seven bones showed evidence of burning.

The posthole line produced 10 fragments, a pelvis, femur, and tibia belonging to rodent; a vertebra, tibio-fibula and metapodial belonging to an amphibian and 3 herring vertebrae.

Phase 3
Both toad *(Bufo bufo)* and herring were identified in the remains from the phase 3 sub-rectangular ditch arrangement (Table 11). The presence of toad was determined by a pelvis although several amphibian limb bones and a vertebra that it was not possible to identify to species were also present. The 3 herring bones are all vertebra.

Discussion

There is nothing to suggest that the rodent and amphibian remains are anthropogenic in nature and they most likely represent natural casualties. In contrast, it is probable that the lagomorph, galliform, herring, large gadid and flatfish formed part of the diet of the inhabitants. The earliest evidence for the introduction of rabbit to Britain is from Rayleigh Castle, Essex (Hinton, 1912–13) between the Conquest and 1220, although hare is often found on sites of this period. Domestic fowl, herring, large gadid and flatfish were often eaten at this time although it is not possible to determine if the fish from Northfleet were imported to the site in a fresh or cured form.

Marine shells
by Greg Campbell

The site produced a small assemblage of 108 identifiable marine shells. Almost all are of oyster (*Ostrea edulis*), with eight shells of edible whelk (*Buccinum undatum*) and two fragments of mussel shell, probably edible or common mussel (*Mytilus edulis*). Preservation was fair, although degradation has led to crumbling at the margins of the oysters and to softening and breakage of the more solid shells. More delicate shells such as mussel are likely to be under-represented.

The oysters come in a wide size range, from about 50 mm up to an estimated 200 mm on one incomplete shell, but the approximate mean length of 70 mm is somewhat small. The range of shapes is also wide, with many elongated due to crowding. The original surface survived on almost all the shells, indicating that the oysters were not heavily infested with barnacles but were supporting a population of shell-boring worms in some cases. These characteristics in combination with the inconsistent and elongated shell shapes indicate that the oysters were gathered by regular removal of nearly all oysters from beds that were then left to rejuvenate naturally.

Virtually all the shells were recovered from ditch fills with few in the pits or the hollows. No deposit seems to have been especially rich in shells although there did seem to be a concentration in the vicinity of the south-east edge of the pylon base. It can be concluded that the contribution of shellfish to the diet of the occupants of the site was small but significant.

Charred plant remains
by Ruth Pelling

Introduction

A series of samples were taken for the retrieval of charred plant remains. A total of 14 samples were available, of which 11 contained sufficient remains (greater than 100 items) to merit further analysis. Table 12 shows the origin and phasing of the analysed samples. The original volume of deposit processed ranged from 5 to 40

Table 12: Analysed environmental samples – source and phasing

Sample No.	Context	Type	Phase
1	508	Fill of beam slot 509	1
2	513	Fill of feature 554 (same as 531)	1
3	523	Fill of ditch 525	3
5	599	Fill of pit/posthole 598	1
6	558	Fill of feature 560	1
7	559	Fill of feature 560	1
9	537	Fill of ditch 578	2
11	651	Fill of gully 652	2
12	656	Fill of feature 560	1
14	760	Fill of feature 793	2
25	762	Fill of feature 560	1

litres. Samples were processed by bulk water flotation and flots collected onto a 500 μm mesh. The samples analysed are all of late 11th- to mid 12th-century date (phases 1 – 3).

Methodology

Dried flots were sorted under a binocular microscope at ×10 to ×20 magnification. Any identifiable and quantifiable plant remains were retrieved for identification. Identifications were based on morphological characteristics and by comparison with modern reference material held at the Oxford University Museum. Nomenclature and taxonomic order follow Clapham, Tutin and Moore (1989).

Results

All samples analysed were dominated by cereal grain, notably short grained free-threshing *Triticum* sp. (wheat). In total wheat grain forms 78% of the identifiable cereal grain. The grain was generally poorly preserved and the *Triticum* sp. grain in particular was bubbly and tarry, consistent with it being subjected to high temperatures. *Hordeum vulgare* (barley) grain was present but was particularly badly preserved and very abraded. While it is not thought that barley formed a very major component of the assemblages its generally poor condition suggests that it is likely to be under-represented. Of the identifiable grains it forms only 6.8%. The barley represented appears to be a hulled variety. *Avena* sp. (oats) were present in larger numbers (13% of identifiable grain), although they are often more easily recognised by their long narrow shape, even after high degrees of distortion. The ratio of oats to barley may actually, therefore, be closer than it appears. Finally, *Secale cereale* (rye) is also present, although only rarely represented by grain, but more frequently by rachis.

Chaff was poorly represented, as is generally the case with free-threshing cereals, for a number of possible reasons including reduced chance of coming into contact with fire. Sufficient wheat rachis was present to demonstrate the presence of a hexaploid, *Triticum aestivum* (bread wheat) type wheat. No tetraploid *Triticum turgidum* (rivet wheat) was present. A single *Triticum spelta* (spelt wheat) glume base is out of place in this context (sample 25) and is likely to be derived from Roman features within the immediate environment. Occasional basal rachis nodes suggest whole ears of wheat or rye may be represented. There is only very limited evidence for straw (4 culm nodes).

Pulses are present in all the samples analysed and in really quite significant numbers given the differential survival rate of pulses and cereal grains. The majority of pulses are in a poor state of preservation being much abraded and lacking the characteristic testa/hila. These pulses were recorded simply as *Vicia/Pisum* sp. (bean/vetch/pea).

Occasional identifiable pulses include a possible *Pisum sativum* (pea), a *Vicia* cf. *faba* (broad bean) and eight *Vicia sativa* subsp. *sativa* (cultivated vetch).

Other species of economic significance include one seed of *Linum usitassimum* (flax) and occasional fragments of *Corylus avellana* (hazelnut) and *Corylus avellana/Prunus* sp. (hazel/sloe, plum etc.).

The majority of the weeds are common arable/ruderal species, well represented on southern British sites at this time. Winter germinating annual weeds which may be associated with winter sown cereals are represented, for example by *Agrostemma githago* (corn cockle), *Anthemis cotula* (stinking mayweed), *Lithospermum arvense* (corn gromwell), *Vicia sativa* (vetch) and *Centaurea cyanus* (corn flower). Conversely, some species are more associated with spring sown cereal crops such as oats, and garden crops such as the pulses. They include *Stellaria media* (chickweed), *Chenopodium album* (fat hen), *Atriplex* sp. (orache), *Fallopia convolvulus* (black bindweed), and *Tripleurospermum inodorum* (scentless mayweed) although some will also do well in winter cereals. *Centaurea cyanus* is regarded by James Greig as becoming abundant quite suddenly after about AD1200 (Greig 1988), although it is recorded from the later Saxon period onwards. Along with *Rumex acetosella* (sheeps sorrel) it is characteristic of rather acid and sandy soils such as would support a rye crop when many other cereals would fail. Its sudden expansion has therefore been related to an increased cultivation of rye (ibid). A greater number of the species present are more commonly associated with clay soils, including *Odontites verna* (red barstia), *Galium aparine* (goosegrass), *Anthemis cotula* and *Anthemis arvensis* (corn chamomile). An unusual find was a seed, still with some flesh, of *Juniperus communis* (juniper), the berry of which is best known for its use in making gin. In the south of England juniper is a species of hot, dry, calcium rich soils and is characteristic of the sunny bare chalk downlands.

Discussion

The charred plant remains generally suggest mixed cereal assemblages containing both cereal product and processing by-product. Such material is often re-deposited within archaeological features as rubbish or amongst the debris of fires or ovens. The cereal evidence is dominated by bread type wheat. Rivet wheat is not represented, although its presence elsewhere in the 11th and 12th century is known (Moffett 1991). The remaining cereals, barley, oats and rye, were well established by the early medieval period in much of southern Britain.

An important find is that of the cultivated vetch (*Vicia sativa* subsp. *sativa*) from a phase I deposit. The first documentary evidence for *Vicia sativa* subsp. *sativa* is from the early 13th century and suggests an association of vetches with chalk and limestone (Campbell 1988). Archaeological records now suggest its cultivation from at least the 12th century (Campbell 1994). The Northfleet examples therefore provide evidence of the cultivation of vetch as early as the late 11th or early 12th century. While the drift geology in the immediate area is Pleistocene sands and gravels, the underlying geology through much of the wider area is chalk, which fits with the historically suggested geological distribution. The cultivation of legumes appears to have formed an important component of the archaeological economy of Kent from early times (Campbell, pers comm; author's own observations) and it is perhaps not unexpected that the cultivation of vetch was also adopted at an early date.

The weeds suggest a significant exploitation of calcareous clay soils, despite the drift geology of Pleistocene gravels, although there is also evidence of the cultivation of the light sandy soils of the gravels. This suggests either that pockets of clay soils were present within the gravels in the immediate area, or that the chalk downlands to the south of the site were being exploited.

The archive

The archive has been microfilmed and a copy has been deposited with the National Archaeological Record. The records and finds are currently in the keeping of Oxford Archaeological Unit, pending transfer to a suitable long term store in Kent.

Table 13: The charred plant remains

		Sample	1	2	6	7	12	25	5	9	14	11	3
		Context	508	513	558	559	656	762	599	537	760	651	523
		Phase	1	1	1	1	1	1	1	2	2	2	3
		Volume	26	20	5	40	40	20	19	40	40	40	40
		Fraction	100%	100%	100%	100%	100%	100%	100%	100%	12.3%	100%	100%
Triticum sp.	Wheat, free-threshing compact grain		76	62	10	22	222	18	77	63	281	4	91
Triticum sp.	Wheat grain		36	20	5	10	32	5	27	16	124	8	24
Hordeum vulgare	Barley, hulled grain		11	1	2	1	2	2	18	—	—	1	—
Hordeum vulgare	*Barley grain*		13	2	12	4	7	13	3	3	10	3	2
Avena sp.	Oats		6	29	10	9	7	5	13	5	10	11	8
Secale cereale	Rye grain		3	—	—	1	—	—	4	—	1	—	1
Secale cereale/Triticum sp.	Rye/Wheat grain		5	3	—	1	2	—	5	2	—	2	3
Indeterminate	Grain		98	122	53	49	281	52	115	76	160	38	132
Triticum aestivum type	Bread type (hexaploid) wheat rachis		—	—	—	—	1	—	—	—	5	—	7
Triticum sp.	Wheat, free-threshing rachis		—	3	1	2	17	1	9	1	57	6	29
Triticum sp.	Wheat, basal rachis		—	—	—	—	—	—	—	—	—	—	1
Triticum spelta/dicoccum	Spelt wheat glume base		—	—	—	—	—	1	—	—	—	—	—
Secale cereale	Rye rachis		12	—	—	—	—	—	2	—	16	—	11
S. cereale/H. vulgare	Rye/Barley rachis		3	—	1	—	—	1	—	—	—	—	—
Avena sp.	Oats, awn fragment		1	—	—	—	—	—	—	—	—	—	—
Indeterminate	Basal rachis		—	—	1	—	—	—	—	—	2	—	3
Indeterminate	Rachis		10	5	1	1	2	2	4	—	9	—	27
Indeterminate	Detached Embryo		1	—	1	—	2	—	—	—	3	—	—
Cereal size	culm node		—	—	—	—	—	1	—	3	—	—	—
cf. *Pisum sativum*	Pea		—	—	—	—	—	—	—	—	1	—	—
Vicia cf. *faba*	Broad Bean		—	—	—	—	2	—	—	—	—	—	—
Vicia sativa	Cultivated Vetch		—	—	—	—	2	—	—	—	1	—	—
Vicia cf. *sativa*	cf. Cultivated Vetch		1	—	—	—	1	—	—	—	3	—	—
Vicia/Pisum sp.	Vetch/bean/pea		17	6	1	13	85	25	19	5	39	7	5
Linum usitassimum	Flax seed		—	—	—	—	1	—	—	—	—	—	—
Corylus avellana	Hazel nut shell fragments		—	—	—	1	—	—	—	—	—	—	—
Corylus avellana/Prunus sp.	Hazel nut/Sloe, plum etc fragments		—	—	—	—	2	—	—	—	1	—	1
Brassica/Sinapis sp.	—		—	—	—	2	—	—	—	—	—	—	—
Juniperus communis	Juniper		—	—	—	—	1	—	—	—	—	—	—
Silene dioica	Red Campion		—	—	—	—	—	—	—	—	2	—	—
Silene sp.	Campion		3	1	—	—	—	1	—	—	—	—	—

Silene sp.	Campion capsule tips	2	—	—	—	—	—	—	—	—	—	—
Agrostemma githago	Corn Cockle	1	2	—	—	—	—	1	1	—	1	—
cf. *Agrostemma githago*	cf. Corn Cockle	—	—	—	—	—	—	—	—	—	—	—
Stellaria media agg.	Chickweed	2	—	—	—	—	1	—	—	—	—	—
Caryophyllaceae	—	—	—	—	—	—	—	—	—	—	2	—
Chenopodium album	Fat Hen	3	7	—	—	6	—	3	—	—	—	—
Chenopodium sp.	Fat Hen/Goosefoot	—	—	—	—	—	—	—	—	—	—	—
Atriplex sp.	Orache	—	—	—	—	17	1	—	—	—	1	—
Chenopodiaceae	—	6	—	—	—	17	1	1	—	—	1	—
cf. *Anagalis* sp.	Pimpernel	—	—	—	—	—	—	—	—	1	—	—
Vicia/*Lathyrus* sp.	Vetch/Vetchling	11	8	1	4	13	3	11	3	3	3	3
Veronica agrestis	Green Field-speedwell	—	—	—	—	4	—	—	—	—	—	—
Polygonum aviculare agg.	Knotgrass	—	1	2	—	7	1	—	—	—	—	—
Polygonum sp.	—	—	—	—	—	—	—	—	—	—	—	—
Fallopia convolvulus	Black Bindweed	2	1	—	—	—	—	—	—	—	1	—
Rumex acetosella	Sheeps Sorrel	—	—	—	—	—	—	—	1	—	—	—
Rumex sp.	Docks	4	5	—	—	5	4	4	—	17	1	1
Polygonaceae	—	—	2	1	—	5	—	1	—	—	1	—
Lithospermum arvense	Corn Gromwell	—	—	—	—	—	—	—	—	(3)	—	—
Odontites verna/*Euphrasia* sp.	Red barstia/euphrasia	1	1	—	—	—	—	—	—	—	—	—
Plantago major	Plantain	—	—	—	—	—	—	—	—	—	—	—
Plantago lanceolata/*media*	Ribwort/Hoary Plantain	—	—	—	—	—	—	—	—	—	—	—
Galium aparine	Goosegrass Cleavers	1	2	—	—	1	—	—	—	—	—	1
Sambucus nigra	Elder	—	1	—	—	—	—	—	—	—	—	—
Anthemis cotula	Stinking Mayweed	24	3	12	5	22	5	8	19	54*	21	62
Anthemis arvensis	Corn Chamomile	—	—	—	—	—	1	—	—	—	—	—
Centaurea cyanus	Cornflower	2	—	—	—	6	1	—	—	2	—	—
Centaurea sp.	Knapweed, Cornflower	5	1	2	1	—	1	1	—	1	—	—
Lapsana communis	Nipplewort	2	—	—	—	—	—	—	—	—	—	—
Tripleurospermum inodorum	Scentless Mayweed	1	—	—	—	1	1	—	—	1	—	1
Compositae	—	1	—	—	—	1	—	—	—	1	1	1
Carex sp.	Sedges	—	—	—	—	—	—	—	—	—	1	—
Bromus subsect *Eubromus*	Brome grass	2	—	—	—	—	—	—	—	1	—	—
Lolium perenne type	Rye Grass	3	—	—	—	—	—	—	—	1	—	—
Gramineae (small)	Grass, small seeded	1	—	—	—	—	?	—	—	1	—	—
Indet catkin	—	—	—	—	—	—	—	1	—	—	—	—
Indet seed	—	8	3	6	4	28	7	5	—	7	1	—
Total		378	291	122	130	802	156	332	194	765	155	414>

Items quantified are seed, nutlet etc unless otherwise stated
* seed cluster
() silica seed

Bibliography   Blair, W J, 1994 *Anglo-Saxon Oxfordshire*, Oxford

Blinkhorn, P W, in prep, The Trials of Being A Utensil: Vessel Use at the Medieval Hamlet of West Cotton, Northamptonshire, *Medieval Ceramics*

Boessneck, J, 1969 Osteological Differences in Sheep (*Ovis aries* Linné) and Goat (*Capra hircus* Linné), in DR Brothwell and ES Higgs (eds) *Science in Archaeology*, London, 331–358

Boyle, A, and Early, R, 1998 *Excavations at Springhead Roman Town, Southfleet, Kent*, Oxford Archaeological Unit Occasional Paper No. 1, Oxford

Burnham, B C, and Wacher, J S, 1990 *The 'small towns' of Roman Britain*, London

Campbell, B M S, 1988 The diffusion of vetches in Medieval England, *Economic History Review* (2nd series), London **41**, 193–208

Campbell, G, 1994 The preliminary archaeobotanical results from Anglo-Saxon West Cotton and Raunds, in J Rackham (ed) *Environment and Economy in Anglo-Saxon England*, CBA Research Report **89**, London, 65–82

Chapelot, J, and Fossier, R, 1980 *The Village and House in the Middle Ages*, Hachette, France

Clapham, A R, Tutin, T G, and Moore, D M, 1989 *Flora of the British Isles* (3rd ed.), Cambridge

Clutton-Brock, J, 1976 The animal resources, in D M Wilson (ed.) *The Archaeology of Anglo-Saxon England*, Cambridge, 373–392

Detsicas, A, 1983 *The Cantiaci*, Gloucester

Dumbreck, W V, 1959 The Lowry of Tonbridge, *Archaeol. Cantiana* **lxxii**, 138–147

Edwards, K. J, 1974 Recent developments in the study of place names and the Anglo-Saxon settlement, *Archaeol. Cantiana* **lxxxviii**, 81–86

Everitt, A, 1986 *Continuity and Colonization: The Evolution of Kentish Settlement*, Leicester

Glass, H J, 1999 (ed) Archaeology of the Channel Tunnel Rail Link, *Archaeol. Cantiana* **cxix**, 189–220

Grant, A, 1982 The Use of Tooth Wear as a Guide to the Age of Domestic Ungulates, in R Wilson, C Grigson and S Payne (eds) *Ageing and Sexing Animal Bones from Archaeological Sites*, BAR Brit. Ser. **109**, Oxford

Greig, J, 1988 Traditional cornfield weeds – where are they now? *Plants Today*, Nov–Dec 1988, London, 183–191

Halstead, P, 1985 A study of Mandibular teeth from Romano-British contexts at Maxey, in F Pryor and C French, *Archaeology and environment in the lower Welland valley. Clo. 1.* EAA Report **27**, 219–223

Hamerow, H, 1993 *Excavations at Mucking Volume 2: the Anglo-Saxon settlement.* English Heritage Archaeological Report no **21**, London

Hasted, E, 1797 *The History and Topographical Survey of the County of Kent* (12 vols)

Hinton, M A C, 1912–1913 On the remains of vertebrate animals found in the middens of Rayleigh castle, *Essex Natur* **17**, 16–21

Hiscock, R H, 1969 The Road Between Dartford, Gravesend and Strood, *Archaeol. Cantiana* **lxxxiii**, 229–248

Leeds, E T, 1913 *The Archaeology of the Anglo-Saxon Settlements*, Oxford

Maltby, J M, 1979 *The animal bones from Exeter 1971–1975*, Exeter Archaeological Reports Vol **2**, Sheffield

McCarthy, M R, and Brooks, C M, 1988 *Medieval Pottery in Britain AD 900–1600*, Leicester

Medlycott, M, 1996 A medieval farm and its landscape: excavations at Stebbingford, Felsted 1993, *Essex Archaeology and History* **27**, 102–81

Moffett, L, 1991 The archaeobotanical evidence for free-threshing tetraploid wheat in Britain, in E. Hajnalova (ed) *Palaeoethnobotany and Archaeology, Acta Interdisciplinaria Archaeologica*, Tomus **VII**, Nitra, 233–244

Mynard, D C, 1973 Medieval Pottery from Dartford, *Archaeol Cantiana* **lxxxviii**, 187–200

Newman, J, 1969 West Kent and the Weald in N Pevsner (ed.) *The Buildings of England*, Middlesex

O'Connor, T P, 1982 *Animal bones from Flaxengate, Lincoln c 870–1500*, CBA for the Lincoln Archaeological Trust, London

Payne, S, 1973 Kill-Off Patterns in Sheep and Goats: The Mandibles from Asvan Kale, *Anatolian Studies: Journal of the British Institute of Archaeology at Ankara*, Vol **xxiii** 281–303

Pearce, J E, Vince, A G, and Jenner, M A, 1985 *A Dated Type-Series of London Medieval Pottery Part 2: London-type Ware* LAMAS Special Paper **6**

Philp, B, and Chenery, M, 1997 *A Roman site at Springhead (Vagniacae) near Gravesend*, Kent Special Subjects Series No **9**, Canterbury

Pratt, S, Riddler, I D, and Gardiner, M (forthcoming) The early medieval settlement, in J Rady, A Hicks, I Riddler and S Pratt, Roads to the Past: the Monkton Landscapes, Canterbury Archaeological Trust Occasional Papers (forthcoming)

Prummel, W, and Frisch, H-J, 1986 A Guide for the distinction of species, sex and body size in bones of sheep and goat, *Journal of Archaeological Science* **xiii**, 567–77

Rigold, S E, and Fleming, A J, 1973 Eynsford Castle: The Moat and Bridge, *Archaeol Cantiana* **lxxxviii**, 87–116

Serjeantson, D, 1996 The Animal Bones, in S Needham and T Spence (eds) *Runnymede Bridge Research Excavations, Volume* **2**. *Refuse and Disposal at Area 16 East Runnymede*, London, 194–223

Silver, I A, 1969 The Ageing of Domestic Animals, in D R Brothwell and E S Higgs (eds), *Science in Archaeology*, London, 283–303

Smith, C R, 1848 Discovery of Anglo-Saxon Remains at Northfleet, Kent, *The Journal of the British Archaeological Association* **iii**, London, 233–241

Smith, V T C, 1997 The Roman road at Springhead Nurseries, *Archaeol. Cantiana* **cxvii**, 51–68

Tester, P J, 1969 An Anglo-Saxon Cemetery at (Orpington), *Archaeol. Cantiana* **lxxxiii**, 125–150

Trow-Smith, R, 1957 *A History of British Livestock Husbandry 1700–1900*, London

URS 1999 Northumberland Bottom: archaeological excavation interim report, prepared for Union Railways (South) Ltd by the Museum of London Archaeology Service

URS 2000 Area 440 North of Westenhanger Castle: post-excavation assessment report (draft version), prepared for Union Railways (South) Ltd by the Canterbury Archaeological Trust

Veale, E M, 1957 The Rabbit in England, *The Agricultural History Review* **5**, 85–90

Vince, A G, 1985 The Saxon and Medieval Pottery of London: A review, *Medieval Archaeology* **29**, 25–93

Von den Driesch, A, 1976 A Guide to the Measurement of Animal bones from Archaeological Sites, *Peabody Museum Bulletin* **1**, Harvard University

Wallenberg, J K, 1934 *The Place-names of Kent*, Uppsala, Sweden

Wilkinson D (ed) 1992 *Oxford Archaeological Unit Field Manual* 2nd edition